The Stories of the Old Testament
A Catholic's Guide

The STORIES of the OLD TESTAMENT

A CATHOLIC'S GUIDE

JIM CAMPBELL

LOYOLAPRESS.

CHICAGO

LOYOLAPRESS.

3441 N. ASHLAND AVENUE
CHICAGO, ILLINOIS 60657
(800) 621-1008
WWW.LOYOLABOOKS.ORG

Nihil Obstat
Reverend Robert L. Tuzik, PhD
Censor Deputatus
May 13, 1999

Imprimatur
Most Reverend Raymond E. Goedert, MA, STL, JCL
Vicar General
Archdiocese of Chicago
May 24, 1999

The *Nihil Obstat* and *Imprimatur* are official declarations that a book is free of doctrinal and moral error. No implication is contained therein that those who have granted the *Nihil Obstat* and *Imprimatur* agree with the content, opinions, or statements expressed. Nor do they assume any legal responsibility associated with publication.

The Scripture quotations contained herein are from the New Revised Standard Version Bible: Catholic Edition, copyright © 1993 and 1989 by the Division of Christian Education of the National Council of the Churches of Christ in the U.S.A. Used by permission. All rights reserved.

Map of the Fertile Crescent (page 15) used by permission of Peter Siu.

Cover illustration © Rob Colvin/Veer

Cover and interior design: Kathryn Seckman Kirsch

Library of Congress Cataloging-in-Publication Data
Campbell, Jim, 1941–
  The stories of the Old Testament : a Catholic's guide / Jim Campbell.
    p. cm.
  ISBN-13: 978-0-8294-2470-6
  ISBN-10: 0-8294-2470-9
  1. Bible stories, English—O.T. 2. Catholic Church—Doctrines. I. Title.
  BS550.3.C36 2007
  221.9'505—dc22
                                              2006039355

Printed in the United States of America
07 08 09 10 11 12 Versa 10 9 8 7 6 5 4 3 2 1

For my grandchildren,
who will be living the faith in the new millennium

CONTENTS

Introduction
READING THE OLD TESTAMENT

A great family project for a rainy day is for parents and grandparents to gather with their children and grandchildren and look through picture albums that tell their family's history. The pictures will reveal faces from the past, which in turn will lead to stories of when the picture was taken and what was happening at the time. Looking at the pictures, our children and grandchildren will discover faces that look familiar, because the person in the picture looks very much like them. In the process, they will begin to understand that they are part of a larger family that extends back in time. They may also realize that they are part of the process of how the family will grow into the future. They will come away with a sense of connection in time and space.

The Stories of the Old Testament is written with this purpose in mind. This helpful guide introduces many of the important people and events that helped form our Catholic faith. We may have some general idea of the more famous Old Testament figures, as their stories have been told, and distorted, in movies and books, but for the most part, we have ignored our ancestors in faith. When we read of them, we will discover that their struggles are like our own. They are heroes, saints, and sinners. They faced successes and failures, living in their own enclaves of faith in a pluralistic world.

The Stories of the Old Testament consists of one hundred readings covering important stories, major figures, and central themes of the Old Testament. Most of these readings span one or two chapters of an Old Testament book. Each reading is a substantial portion of Scripture, yet each is short enough to complete in one sitting. The book itself may be read in a few sittings to get an overview of the Old Testament; then it may be used with the Bible as a daily guide to reading the Old Testament. The short essays summarize some of the ideas found in the readings. However, there is no substitute for actually reading the texts themselves.

Some Catholics may ask why the Old Testament is important. We have the New Testament and the stories of Jesus; shouldn't that be enough? The Catholic Church addressed this issue in the documents of Vatican II. The church teaches that the Old Testament is "a storehouse of sublime teaching on God, and of sound wisdom on human life, as well as a wonderful treasury of prayers" (*Catechism of the Catholic Church*, 122). We believe, furthermore, that these ancient texts still speak to modern people. They are inspired by God and reveal God. The church also teaches that the "patriarchs, prophets and certain other Old Testament figures have been and always will be honored as saints in all the Church's liturgical traditions" (*Catechism of the Catholic Church*, 61).

One resource of particular importance is the *Catechism of the Catholic Church*. References to the *Catechism* (abbreviated *CCC*) can be found at the end of the guides to many of the readings in this book. These references point to paragraphs in the *Catechism* that relate to the theme of the Old Testament reading. They remind us that we read the Bible within the church, as Catholics. They also show us in an especially practical way that our Christian faith is rooted in the faith of the people of Israel.

While there is much to learn and experience about the Old Testament, *The Stories of the Old Testament* is a good start. Hopefully, you will continue to read the Old Testament. It is important to read *about* the Old Testament as well. Some good books are listed in the Suggested Reading section.

The Stories of the Old Testament unlocks the doors of this storehouse of sublime teaching, wisdom, and prayers. It invites you into the great story of God's relationship with the people of Israel, a relationship completed in Jesus Christ. It is a story that continues today and speaks to all of us.

The STORIES *of the* OLD TESTAMENT

A CATHOLIC'S GUIDE

About: The Pentateuch

The first twenty-eight readings in this book are taken from the Pentateuch, the first five books of the Bible, which relates the stories of creation and the early history of Israel. It is fitting that these readings make up more than a quarter of this book, because the Pentateuch tells the central stories of Israel. Genesis relates the stories of creation and of the great patriarchs Abraham, Isaac, Jacob, and Joseph. Exodus tells of God's deliverance of his people from oppression in Egypt and of the covenant between God and Israel. The books of Leviticus, Numbers, and Deuteronomy describe the Law—the rules and commandments that the people were given as their share in the covenant relationship.

The stories told in the Pentateuch take God's people to the threshold of their possession of the Promised Land. The rest of the Old Testament takes place in the land of Israel. The *historical books* tell about the era of the judges and kings and about the eventual division of the kingdom. The *prophetic books* recount the people's covenant failures and God's response. The *writings*, which include the psalms, the wisdom books, and later histories, record Israel's profound religious and spiritual reflections.

But the foundation of Israel's history is the Pentateuch, particularly the stories told in Genesis and Exodus. The readings that follow tell of the "mighty acts" of God performed to create a people who would be his instrument of salvation for the world.

1

The Days of Creation
READ GENESIS 1:1–2:4

God said, "Let there be light"; and there was light.
GENESIS 1:3

The first chapters of Genesis tell of God creating the heavens and the earth; filling the earth with plant, animal, and human life; and proclaiming it all good. The story was written when the Jewish people lived in the city of Babylon between the years 597 BC and 539 BC. Babylonian armies had invaded Judah and had captured and deported the leading Jewish families. Jewish aristocrats now farmed to feed themselves. They knew that they had failed God.

In Babylon, stories about the Babylonian gods tempted the Jewish people. The Babylonian story of creation is filled with violent images. It says that humans were created from the bad blood of a bad god to be slaves to the gods. In spite of its violence, this story was attractive to the Jewish people in exile. They had lost the land that God had given them. To the rest of the world, this meant that their God had lost. Were the Babylonian deities more powerful?

Jewish religious leaders wrote Genesis 1:1–2:4 to counter these influences. In the Genesis account, God lovingly speaks, and life comes into being. The first man and woman are blessed and meant to live in harmony with nature.

The Genesis creation story is structured like a workweek, since creation is God's work. On day one, light is created and is separated from the darkness. On day two, God divides the waters with a dome called the sky. Earth and vegetation are created on day three. On day four, God creates the sun and the moon and the stars. On day five, God fills the waters with living creatures and the air with birds. On day six, God creates the human family: "So God created humankind in his image, in the image of God he created them; male and female he created them" (Genesis 1:27).

Human beings are not created out of the bad blood of a bad god. They are made in the image of the God who blesses and who calls them to bless one another. The man and the woman are created equal and are called to multiply and fill the earth.

On the seventh day, God rests.

2

Adam and Eve
READ GENESIS 2:4–24

The man said,
"This at last is bone of my bones
and flesh of my flesh."
GENESIS 2:23

In the second creation story in the Bible, written much earlier than Genesis 1:1–2:4, God is pictured as shaping a man from the soil of the ground. Adam's name probably comes from the Hebrew word *adamah*, which means "earth." God "breathed into his nostrils the breath of life" (Genesis 2:7), but God did not simply breathe air into the man; God shared divine life with him. In this telling of the story, the author shows how special human beings are. Every person is sacred, because every person lives in the breath of God.

God creates a garden, usually translated as "paradise." God gives the man trees with every kind of fruit to cultivate and take care of. The only thing that is forbidden is the fruit of the tree of the knowledge of good and evil. The tree is "of the knowledge of good and evil," but this does not mean that it helps people know everything or helps them tell the difference between good and evil. God has already given the man the ability to do this. What "the knowledge of good and evil" seems to mean here is the power *to decide* what is good and what is evil.

The man is alone, and God sees that he is incomplete. God puts the man to sleep, and from his rib God creates a woman to be his partner. The woman is not inferior to the man. Adam recognizes the woman as "bone of my bones and flesh of my flesh." He names her Eve, meaning "the mother of all living" (Genesis 3:20). The author notes that this creates the foundation for marriage, where the husband and the wife will leave their families to create the most intimate relationship with one another.

Creation is now complete, with the man and the woman living naked but unashamed—a sign of their intimacy and harmony—in the world that God has given them to nurture and to grow in.

CCC, 369–79: Man and woman

3

The Fall of Adam and Eve

READ GENESIS 3

*She took of its fruit and ate; and she also gave some to her
husband, who was with her, and he ate.*

GENESIS 3:6

Genesis 3 tells how Adam and Eve's intimacy with God and with each other is disrupted. The serpent enters the scene. The serpent represents anything that can separate a person from God. The woman, with the man as her silent partner, speaks to the serpent. They examine the possibility of disobeying God. Will Adam and Eve accept God's moral order and trust in his love?

The serpent asks the man and the woman if they can eat from every tree in the garden. The woman replies that God forbade them to eat from the tree in the middle of the garden. The serpent misleads them. He tells them that the reason God forbade them to eat this fruit is that it will give them God's own knowledge of good and evil. Things are always more tempting when they are forbidden, and this is obviously the case here. The woman takes the fruit, eats it, and gives some to the man, who does the same.

The consequences are immediate. The intimacy between Adam and Eve is shattered. They become ashamed of their nakedness. Genesis says "they sewed fig leaves together and made loincloths for themselves" (Genesis 3:7). They also lose their intimacy with God: hearing God walking in the garden, the man and the woman hide in fear.

When God calls to them, they tell him they are naked. Who told you so, God asks, and continues, "Have you eaten from the tree of which I commanded you not to eat?" (Genesis 3:11).

Adam and Eve now distrust one another. The man takes no responsibility for his actions but blames the woman. The woman blames the snake. The man and the woman have learned what it means to live outside of God's moral order. It leads to mistrust, blame, and broken relationships.

The man and the woman have discovered that sin causes suffering: the world now becomes a place demanding hard work. The woman loses her equal partnership with her husband, and he will dominate her. The man must work to feed them. The woman must have her children in pain. They must leave the garden of paradise. Another consequence is that the human family will be born into original sin as a result of the sin of our first parents.

God gives Adam and Eve a sign of protection. They receive garments of skin before they are expelled from paradise. Life without suffering—symbolized by a garden of intimacy and sharing for all and with all—is over. Anyone who thinks that humans can create such a place without respecting God's moral order learns the same lesson Adam and Eve learned. The result can only be disaster.

CCC, 396–405: Man's first sin

4

Cain and Abel

READ GENESIS 4

Am I my brother's keeper?
GENESIS 4:9

Adam and Eve have two sons, Cain and Abel. Cain and Abel's story shows the deepening effect of sin.

The story is simple. Cain and Abel both offer God the best they have in sacrifice. Abel's offering is accepted. Cain's offering is not, and he is angry and discouraged. While early Christian writers describe Abel as being more righteous than Cain, Genesis does not say this. God accepts the offering of the younger brother for his own reasons. This pattern is repeated in the Bible with the choice of Abraham over his relatives, Isaac over Ishmael, Jacob over Esau, and Joseph and David over their older brothers.

Cain's hurt feelings turn into deep hatred of Abel. Cain believes God has insulted him. God tells Cain to continue living in relationship with him and others. Unfortunately, sin is like a beast lurking at the door, ready to master the heart of Cain. Cain refuses to make the choice of mastering this beast.

Cain goes into the field with Abel and kills him. We see here the growing effect of sin. It begins with blame in the story of Adam and Eve. It now advances to murder in the story of Cain and Abel.

Cain hopes his actions will be a secret, but nothing is secret from God. God, looking for Abel, calls on Cain. Baldly lying to God, Cain replies, "I do not know; am I my brother's keeper?" God punishes Cain for his actions.

Cain's punishment is to become a restless wanderer. He complains that he is without protection. God listens and responds to his prayer, setting a mark upon him so that he will be safe. Note that this "mark on Cain" is a sign of God's mercy and protection, not a mark of shame.

We are all tempted by the thought that the good fortune of others means a failure on our part. This can lead, as it did with Cain, to jealous criticism and envy. This not only hurts others but also, as with Cain, leads to self-destruction.

CCC, 401: The universality of sin

5

Noah and the Flood
READ GENESIS 6–9

Go into the ark, you and all your household,
for I have seen that you alone are righteous.
GENESIS 7:1

The story of Noah is told to illustrate how deeply the human family has fallen into sinfulness. Sin is now so universal that a troubled God decides to complete the work of destruction that the human family has begun (Genesis 6:13). However, God sees that Noah is a good man and decides that humanity will survive through Noah's family. God tells Noah to build an ark, which God will use to save Noah's family and members of the animal kingdom. God is pained by and disappointed in humankind, but in his mercy he will save the human family through Noah.

Noah builds the ark and, following God's instructions, loads himself, his family, and the animals into it. God closes the door of the ark, showing his care for all inside and for the future human family.

The flood comes, joining the waters of the sky with the waters on the earth. As the ark floats higher, everything beneath it drowns. For forty days and nights it rains. It is another 150 days before the water recedes.

Then God remembers Noah. In his remembering, God begins the process of re-creation: "And God made a wind blow over the earth, and the waters subsided" (Genesis 8:1). Noah sends out birds to see if it is safe to disembark. He first sends a raven, then a dove. The second time he sends the dove, it returns with an olive branch in its beak. God then tells Noah to leave the ark with his family and all of the animals and begin to repopulate the earth.

God makes a covenant with all the living beings. Although the evil in the human heart continues to flourish, God promises that never again will he destroy the earth in a flood. The sign of this covenant, or promise, is the rainbow.

The story of Noah shows how, even in the face of terrible sin, God wants to save the human family.

CCC, 56–58: The covenant with Noah

6

The Tower of Babel

Therefore it was called Babel, because there the LORD
confused the language of all the earth.

GENESIS 11:9

We are always curious as to why things are the way they are. Why is the sky blue? How does water freeze? Why does the moon shine more brightly on some nights than on others? The story of the Tower of Babel could have begun as an answer to such a question: Why do people speak in so many diverse languages?

The setting of the story is the city of Babylon, the city to which the Jews were brought after the Babylonian conquest of Judah in 597–587 BC. Babylon was a city built of bricks and mortar. There was no natural stone in Babylonia (present-day Iraq), so people made bricks of clay baked in kilns.

The inspiration for the story of the tower may have come from the shape of the pagan temples in Babylon. The principal temples of worship in Babylonia were the ziggurats, pyramid-like structures built to resemble mountains. There was usually a sanctuary on the ground level of the ziggurat that was matched

13

by a sanctuary at the top, where the deities were worshiped. The believers climbed in procession to the top of the pyramid to pray to their gods.

The story of the Tower of Babel begins with the statement that "The whole earth had one language and the same words" (Genesis 11:1). Now as the people moved east, they found a place to build a city on the Mesopotamian plain, in Shinar, the name for Babylonia (Genesis 11:2). The people said they would settle there and move no further: "Then they said, 'Come, let us build ourselves a city, and a tower with its top in the heavens, and let us make a name for ourselves; otherwise we shall be scattered abroad upon the face of the whole earth'" (Genesis 11:4).

Making a name for themselves meant being independent of God and not following his plan that they multiply and fill the earth (Genesis 9:7).

God came down to see the city and discovered the people's plan. God was not pleased to see that the people did not wish to grow but wanted to control their own destiny and use their creative talents only for themselves. God decided to confuse their language so they could not understand one another. As a result, the people scattered, and God's will for the human race to grow and multiply moved forward (Genesis 11:9).

God made sure that the people would be more than a single isolated community. God intends for people to use their creativity to complete the earth, not to selfishly build their own private worlds; God does not support a community in which people live in cliques. The community that God wants on earth is one that cares about the entire world.

CCC, 57: Social disunity

About: The Fertile Crescent

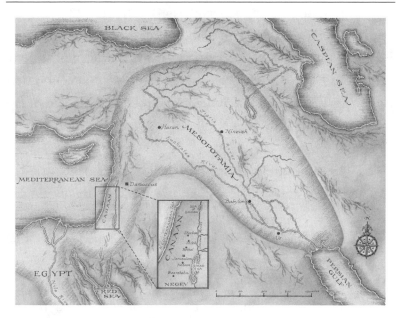

As we begin to explore the historical developments of the Old Testament, beginning with the story of Abraham, it is important that we look at the geography of the Middle East. We especially have to look at what is known as the Fertile Crescent.

The arc of land that makes up the Fertile Crescent begins at the point where the Tigris and Euphrates rivers flow into the Persian Gulf. As we go up the rivers in an arc sweeping to the left, moving through present-day Iraq, we find some of the cities that grew up by these rivers. The ancient cities of the Sumerians were the first to display signs of what would become Western civilization. In the time of Abraham, the important cities were Ur and Haran. Later this area supported the Assyrian Empire (1900–612 BC), the Babylonian Empire (606–536 BC), and the Persian Empire (648–330 BC).

We continue the sweep west to the Mediterranean Sea. At the juncture of the sea and the land, we move directly south, through Canaan, the land located between Syria and Egypt, where the Israelites settled. At the southernmost tip of Canaan is the Sinai Desert, where present-day Israel borders Egypt. In Egypt, a great civilization arose with the aid of the resources of the Nile River and dominated the region for two thousand years.

Civilizations grew up in the Fertile Crescent because the availability of water made agriculture possible. Below the arc of the Tigris-Euphrates River Valley and east of the shoreline communities that developed in Syria is scorched desert that could not support agricultural life.

The availability of water meant that not only agriculture but also trade could be supported. The coastal regions of Syria and Canaan were the only viable trade routes between Egypt in the south, the cities of the Tigris-Euphrates River Valley, and the developing cultures in Asia Minor (present-day Turkey) and Armenia in the north.

Those living in Canaan, then, were always threatened by the ambitious rulers of the surrounding civilizations. When Pharaoh Ramses II (1279–1213 BC) led his conquering armies north, they traveled through Canaan to attack their enemies. As the Assyrians and Babylonians developed civilizations in the Tigris-Euphrates Valley, they attacked south along the Mediterranean through Canaan. King David (c. 1000–962 BC) was able to establish his kingdom and his son Solomon (c. 961–922 BC) was able to expand its borders because they ruled during a temporary power vacuum in the area. Soon the kingdom of David and Solomon was in danger of attack from the north and the south. The Egyptians raided during the reign of Solomon's son Rehoboam (922–915 BC). David and Solomon's kingdom then divided into the kingdom of Israel in the north and the kingdom of Judah in the south. The Assyrians destroyed the kingdom of Israel by 721 BC, and the Babylonians conquered the kingdom of Judah in 597–587 BC.

This was the stage for the historical events that form the background of the Old Testament.

7

The Call of Abraham

READ GENESIS 12

To your offspring I will give this land.
GENESIS 12:7

Now the LORD said to Abram, "Go from your country and your kindred and your father's house to the land that I will show you. I will make of you a great nation, and I will bless you, and make your name great, so that you will be a blessing. I will bless those who bless you, and the one who curses you I will curse; and in you all the families of the earth shall be blessed." (Genesis 12:1–3)

So begins the journey in faith that will lead to the formation of the Hebrew people, their arrival in Canaan, and the foundation of Judaism, Christianity, and Islam. God chooses Abraham and his family. The text does not tell us why Abraham in particular is chosen. Abraham asks no questions, and God does not volunteer any further information.

In Genesis 12–50, the story of God's work in human history leading to Jesus Christ enters into more familiar territory. Up to this point in the book of Genesis, we have read about the creation of the universe and of the human family. The stories of Adam and Eve and of Cain and Abel revealed how the human spirit weakened as the human family acted in more sinful ways. The story of Noah and the flood showed God's distress with a sinful humanity. The story of the Tower of Babel showed the consequences of not wanting to fulfill God's intentions for humankind.

The text now moves from looking at the growing effects of sin to looking at the process of redemption. It begins with the call of a single family, Abraham and Sarah, who emerge as the couple who will be the ancestors of faith for the people of Israel, for Christians, and for Muslims.

Scholars believe that Abraham lived in the period from about 2000 BC to 1500 BC, when civilization was growing in the Tigris-Euphrates Valley. Abraham's family came from the city of Ur, one of the oldest cities in southern Mesopotamia. When he left the city of Ur, he and his followers became nomads. Nomads lived on the fringes of the world of cities, preferring to wander freely with their flocks of sheep and herds of goats and asses. For part of the year they would settle near a village, and for the rest of the year they would travel in search of pastures and water for their animals. Since the climate in the area was dry, they would have to search widely in order to find enough pasture land and water to keep their flocks alive.

Nomads traveled with their animals. They had to travel as efficiently as possible, so they took little baggage and lived in tents. For security, they traveled in groups with other families. They had to know not only where the pastures were that had adequate food and water for their flocks, but also which of the tribes settled in these lands were friendly and which were hostile. Moving into an area, the nomads received permission from local farmers to have their animals graze in recently cut grain fields for a period of time. In return for the grazing, the farmers got the manure that was left behind by the flocks to help fertilize the fields.

This was the life that Abraham, Sarah, and their descendants were called to from the settled life in the cities. Instead of a life that gave them some assurance that things would remain the same, they faced a life of change, uncertainty, and possibility.

While Abraham's future was uncertain, his destination was not. Abraham travels to Shechem, in Canaan, and builds a shrine to worship God. Here God promises Abraham that he will have children who will eventually settle in this land. From there, Abraham, his family, and his flocks travel further, to Bethel and Negeb. In each place he builds a shrine to God.

Abraham and his descendants are models of what it means to live in God's blessing. In Genesis 12–50, blessings are given eighty-eight times. God's blessing cannot be earned but is pure gift. As pure gift, blessings give the person or the people blessed the good things that they need to live to their fullest potential. A blessed person or family is promised material as well as spiritual benefits.

The first chapter of Genesis revealed that God created the universe, said it was very good, and blessed it for the human family to enjoy. Because of sin, people have used God's creation for personal gain instead of sharing it with one another.

So it is important to see that the blessing Abraham and his family received is not for them alone. Rather, "in you all the families of the earth shall be blessed" (Genesis 12:3). Abraham, Sarah, and their descendants (including us, his children in faith) receive abundantly from God. With these blessings comes the responsibility to share with the world that which we have received.

CCC, 59–61: God chooses Abraham

About: Melchizedek

Think of someone who has had an important influence on your life—a teacher, a friend from a foreign country, a beloved grandparent who has died. While you may never see this person again, the memory of his or her influence in your life will last as long as you live. The image of the priest Melchizedek has a similar place in the Bible.

Melchizedek appears in chapter 14 of Genesis. Abraham has been to battle against four kings in Canaan. Upon his return to camp, he is met by Melchizedek, the priest-king of Salem. Salem was located near the site of the future city of Jerusalem. "And King Melchizedek of Salem brought out bread and wine; he was priest of God Most High. He blessed him and said, 'Blessed be Abram by God Most High, maker of heaven and earth; and blessed be God Most High, who has delivered your enemies into your hand!' And Abram gave him one tenth of everything" (Genesis 14:18–20).

Abraham accepts Melchizedek's blessing, which gives him extra strength and shows the world the glory of God.

Melchizedek appears again in Psalm 110, a psalm proclaimed at the coronation of a Davidic king. The psalm announces to the king that "you are a priest forever according to the order of Melchizedek" (110:4). This was prayed to affirm that the Davidic kings in Jerusalem would carry on the priestly tradition, interceding for their people before God.

More important for Christians, Melchizedek appears in Hebrews 7. The writer of Hebrews notes that Melchizedek means "king of righteousness" and "king of peace," two titles that admirably suit Jesus Christ. "Without father, without mother, without genealogy, having neither beginning of days nor end of life, but resembling the Son of God, he remains a priest forever" (Hebrews 7:3). The author of Hebrews argues that since Abraham gave gifts to Melchizedek, Abraham admitted his own inferiority to the king of Salem. Melchizedek is presented in the Scriptures as a king of righteousness and peace. He has no parents or relatives. He is described as an "eternal" priest, without beginning or end. In this way, Melchizedek resembles Jesus, the Son of God. Since he has received the gifts from Abraham, Melchizedek is seen as greater than Abraham and also greater than the priest Aaron (Hebrews 7:1–17). In Hebrews, Melchizedek becomes a model of the eternal priesthood of Christ, "who has been made perfect forever" (Hebrews 7:28).

8

God's Covenant
with Abraham
READ GENESIS 15

To your descendants I give this land,
from the river of Egypt to the great river.
GENESIS 15:18

braham stands before God, facing the future. God had promised that Abraham would be the father of many descendants, but his wife, Sarah, seems unable to have children. So Abraham believes he will die childless and that his steward, Eliezer, will be his heir. God assures Abraham that this will not happen, promising Abraham that he will have a son with Sarah. More than that, the descendants of Abraham will be as numerous as the stars in the sky.

Abraham continues to show his complete trust in God, "and the LORD reckoned it to him as righteousness" (Genesis 15:6). God has Abraham set up a ritual sacrifice. Abraham brings a three-year-old calf, a three-year-old she-goat, a three-year-old ram, a turtledove, and a young pigeon. He then sacrifices them, cutting them in two. He places one half of each animal on one side and the other half on the other.

Abraham is preparing to make a covenant with God. A covenant is an agreement binding two parties that was common in the ancient Near East. The two parties making the covenant would split the animals in two. Then the two parties would walk between the animals. This bound them in the covenant. The split animals symbolized the curse that would fall on either party if one failed to keep his or her part of the agreement.

After preparing the animals, Abraham falls into a deep sleep. This symbolizes a deep state of dreaming, heightening the mystery of God. In his dream, Abraham sees God, symbolized by a smoking firepot and a flaming torch, passing through the divided animals. In this way, God binds himself to Abraham and his descendants. Only God passes through the animals; Abraham does not. Only God has the strength to make the promise that he will be the God of Abraham and Sarah and their descendants forever.

God will never go back on this promise to Abraham and, through Abraham and his descendants, to the whole human family. All believers can hold on to this promise, believing that God fully intends to keep his word. Abraham's act of faith was in response to God's proclaimed word. Abraham accepted God's promise totally, and because of his decision we too live in this unique relationship with God.

CCC, 144–46: Abraham, our father in faith

9

Hagar and Ishmael

READ GENESIS 16; 21

Hagar bore Abram a son, and Abram named his son,
whom Hagar bore, Ishmael.
GENESIS 16:15

As Abraham and Sarah grow older, it seems that God's promise to them has not yet been fulfilled. Sarah is still childless. She suggests to Abraham that he have children by her slave woman Hagar. She allows Hagar to become Abraham's concubine and to bear his child. When Hagar becomes pregnant, she looks down on Sarah, thinking she is now in a better position with Abraham. Sarah objects. Abraham responds by telling Sarah that Hagar is under her control and that Sarah can do with her as she pleases. Sarah treats Hagar harshly, so Hagar runs away.

God meets Hagar and speaks to her as she is running away. He gives her the same promise that he gave Abraham, saying that she will be the mother of a great nation. God calls her by name, recognizing that she is a person who is a child of God—not just a maid or slave, as Abraham and Sarah refer to her. God then commands her to return to Sarah.

Hagar obeys God and gives him the name El-roi, "the God who sees."

Hagar has a son, Ishmael ("God hears"). Hagar and Ishmael live in Abraham's family for a while, until after the birth of Isaac. Sarah, upon seeing Ishmael playing with Isaac, becomes concerned that Isaac might not receive all of Abraham's inheritance. So she demands that Hagar and Ishmael be expelled. Abraham is hesitant, since Ishmael is his son, but Sarah is insistent. Abraham sends Hagar and Ishmael into the desert with some bread and a skin of water. They wander until their water and food are gone. Then Hagar leaves Ishmael under a bush, not wanting to see him die.

Again God sends an angel to Hagar, renewing his promise that Ishmael will become the leader of a great nation. God shows her where they can find water, and they continue their journey. Ishmael grows to become a great warrior and marries a woman his mother finds for him from the land of Egypt. He lives to an old age and becomes the father of twelve tribes who are listed as enemies of the tribes of Israel.

God's care for Hagar is one more instance of God's care for the outcast and for those on the fringes of society. Although powerless, a slave, and foreign born, Hagar became the mother of a nation. Through Ishmael, Abraham is seen as the father of the Arab peoples and the father of faith for Islam. Muslims believe that it was Ishmael, not Isaac, who was intended to be the sacrificial offering for God. They also believe that Ishmael helped Abraham set up the shrine of the Kaaba, the holiest shrine in Islam.

CCC, 332: Angels; 841: Muslims

10

Abraham and Isaac

Do not lay your hand on the boy or do anything to him;
for now I know that you fear God.

GENESIS 22:12

The story of Abraham and Isaac is one of the most famous and moving stories in the Bible. It shows Abraham's readiness to listen to God and to obey.

Abraham has a son by Sarah, as God promised. Abraham's desire for a son was not simply about finding someone to inherit his flocks and belongings. It was also about having his name remembered and carried into the next generation. With the birth of Isaac, he believes that this will happen.

Then, unexpectedly, God sends an angel with the message that Abraham must sacrifice his son Isaac. As bitter as the message is, and as hopeless as it makes Abraham feel, he obeys without hesitation. He gathers his servants and Isaac with wood for the sacrifice and sets out to the appointed place. The last part of the way he goes alone with Isaac, who is made to carry the wood for his own sacrifice. On the way, Isaac asks his father what animal will be sacrificed. Abraham answers that God will provide.

At the place of sacrifice, Abraham makes everything ready to carry out God's commands. Abraham binds Isaac, places him on the altar, and is ready to plunge the knife into him. Then the angel comes again and tells him that God does not want Isaac. The angel provides a ram for sacrifice instead. But because Abraham had been willing to obey, God makes his promises again, with even greater blessing.

It is important to see this story in the context in which it was written. Human sacrifice was common in the Canaanite cities that surrounded the people of Israel. It was even practiced by some people in Israel (2 Kings 16:4; Micah 6:7). Archaeologists have discovered the bones of infants buried under the doorways of homes in Canaanite communities. People thought that the sacrifice of the firstborn would appease the wrath of their gods. The story of Abraham was a response to this. God did not want human sacrifice. Rather, God protects the helpless.

More important in this story, however, is Abraham's readiness to listen to and obey God. He recognized that he must sacrifice whatever future he had envisioned for himself and his family to make God's dreams possible. Abraham turned his future hopes over to God, whose response was to create a greater future than Abraham could have possibly imagined.

CCC, 2572: God's promise and the prayer of faith

11

Sarah

READ GENESIS 12; 21

The LORD dealt with Sarah as he had said,
and the LORD did for Sarah as he had promised.
GENESIS 21:1

The stories of the Bible were written by men who lived in a patriarchal society, so their stories emphasize the actions and decisions of men like Abraham, Isaac, and Jacob. But the decisions and the actions of the women are just as important, since they are also the heirs of the promise that God made to the human family.

Sarah, the wife of Abraham, is a perfect example of this. Sarah traveled the same road as Abraham. Sarah also left her home at the command of God. At times she seemed afraid that her inability to have children would frustrate God's plan. Her faith in God was expressed in her faithfulness to Abraham. God made it very clear that she was necessary to complete his plan. With Abraham, she is the ancestor of many nations.

Sarah is called beautiful and very beautiful. In the Bible, beauty, in almost every case, means not merely physical beauty but also holiness. Sarah was physically attractive as well as holy, living in relationship with God. Sarah was also in need of redemption. She was capable of hurting others, like Hagar, in what she saw as the defense of her family.

The Bible is very honest in telling the stories of our religious ancestors. It tells how God worked through them for our salvation, but it also tells about their sinfulness.

Genesis 12:10–20 relates a story that does not speak well of Abraham but shows how important Sarah was to God's plan. Before the birth of Ishmael and Isaac, Abraham and Sarah move into Egypt. Pharaoh sees Sarah and wants her. He gives Abraham flocks and herds, slaves, and other treasures so that he might have her. Abraham lets Sarah go, saying she is his sister. God's promise to Abraham is threatened when Abraham does not defend Sarah, and he almost loses her as his wife. So God acts in her defense. Plagues come upon Egypt, and Pharaoh learns that Abraham lied to him. Upset and afraid of God, Pharaoh sends Abraham and Sarah away.

Sarah is the mother of the promise. Throughout Scripture she is presented as a hardy and capable woman. Like any man or woman, she was a complex character. She was wise and beautiful. She was fiercely loyal to Abraham and Isaac, sometimes to a fault. She was a flawed person in need of redemption, as we are. She was loved by God and given a special vocation within his plan of salvation.

CCC, 64: Holy women; 145: Abraham's faith

12

Finding a Wife for Isaac
READ GENESIS 24

He took Rebekah, and she became his wife; and he loved her.
GENESIS 24:67

Abraham is old, Sarah is dead, and Isaac is heartbroken. Abraham has to look to Isaac's future, so he calls a servant and charges him with a sacred oath to return to Haran to find a bride for Isaac among Abraham's relatives.

In preparation, the servant gathers gifts. Although he realizes that the journey is under God's guidance, he also realizes that people must prepare themselves. The more people are prepared to do their part, the more effectively God can act in their lives.

When the servant arrives at Haran, he places the search for a bride in God's hands. As a sign to guide his search, he decides that if he meets a woman who will give him water and also water the ten camels he has brought with him, she will be the one. The servant no sooner makes this decision than Rebekah comes to draw water. "The girl was very fair to look upon, a virgin, whom no man had known. She went down to the spring, filled her jar, and came up" (Genesis 24:16).

When she comes up from the spring, the servant asks for a drink. Rebekah not only gives him a drink but also offers to water his camels. In this way, she reveals her character: only a generous and hardworking woman would draw that many gallons of water. The servant then gives Rebekah gifts of earrings and jewelry. He discovers that Rebekah is Abraham's niece. She invites him to spend the night with her family. Hearing this, the servant bows down and worships God for his continuing faithful love.

Laban, Rebekah's brother, impressed by the gifts of jewelry, immediately welcomes Abraham's servant. The servant tells of Abraham's search and of his joy in finding Rebekah. Negotiations are short, and Rebekah is promised to Isaac. The servant, knowing Abraham will die soon, asks to return immediately with Rebekah. It is her decision, and she agrees. Upon the servant and Rebekah's return, Isaac and Rebekah are married. "He took Rebekah, and she became his wife; and he loved her. So Isaac was comforted after his mother's death" (Genesis 24:67).

Rebekah was worthy to be the wife of Isaac. A beautiful woman, she showed herself to be also strong, generous, and hardworking. She made the decision to leave her home to discover whom God had prepared for her as a husband.

The story of Isaac and Rebekah shows that God's will for his people includes the gift of marriage and family. This gift is also the fruit of God's faithfulness and steadfast love.

CCC, 64: Holy women

About: Family in the Old Testament

Family was of primary importance in Old Testament times. Living in Canaan was difficult for a people dependent on the land for grazing animals and growing crops, because the land was dry and not particularly fertile. Families raising grain and grazing animals needed as many laborers as they could get. Large families were essential not only to do the work in the good years, but also to ensure the clan's survival in years of drought and famine. If there were many children, at least some would survive.

In Old Testament times, a family could meet its end in one generation. Many women died in childbirth. Many children died in infancy, a fact that was true into the late nineteenth century. Since so many nations fought over Canaan in Old Testament times, the loss of entire families in war was a common occurrence. Only if there were a large number of family members could there be a likelihood of some survival.

Among the rich and the kings, polygamy was common. A man could marry many wives and have as many children as possible. Since motherhood was held in high esteem, women risked physical pain and possible death to have children.

The structure of the family was primarily patriarchal. The male was the head of the household, and sons were more highly prized than daughters. If a husband died without fathering a son, his brother was to have relations with the husband's widow in an attempt to have a son and raise it in the husband's name (see Deuteronomy 25:5–10). The son inherited the land of his father; if the family had no son, then the closest male relative was the heir. A daughter could inherit from her father if there was no suitable male heir, but she had to marry a man in the tribe so that the father's property would remain in the family (see Numbers 36:1–12).

The foundation of the family was marriage, understood as a covenant between husband and wife (Proverbs 2:17; Malachi 2:14). The family was an extended family, and a household could include other relatives as well as slaves, servants, and resident foreigners. The father had the strongest authority. He arranged his children's marriages and kept the clan faithful to God (Deuteronomy 13:6–11). But children were taught to honor both parents (Exodus 20:12) and to respect equally the dignity of the father and the mother (Proverbs 1:8; 6:20).

CCC, 2201–6: The nature of the family

13

Jacob and Esau
READ GENESIS 25:19–34; 27

Jacob said to his father, "I am Esau your firstborn."
GENESIS 27:19

Isaac and Rebekah were married, but Rebekah was childless for a long time. This theme of childlessness appears throughout the Old Testament and into the New Testament—with Sarah before Rebekah, and Rachel, Hannah, and Elizabeth after her. The childlessness of these women and their continuing faith in God makes the point that God's chosen people exist only because of his actions.

Rebekah finally becomes pregnant after Isaac prays for her and God intervenes (Genesis 25:21). After a long and difficult pregnancy, she gives birth to twin boys. Esau is born first, and Jacob is born clutching at Esau's heel. Esau will become the father of the Edomites, historically enemies of the Israelites. Jacob will become the father of Israel.

As the boys grow, their differences become apparent. Esau, a burly, active boy and Isaac's favorite, is a hunter. Jacob, Rebekah's favorite, is a clever, stay-at-home boy who prefers a shepherd's life.

One day when Esau comes in from the fields starving, he finds Jacob cooking a lentil stew. He asks for some, and Jacob agrees, but only if Esau will sell him his birthright. Esau's birthright as Isaac's firstborn son would give him the right to leadership in the clan and also a double share of Isaac's inheritance. Esau, thinking more of his stomach than his future, agrees. He shows himself to be a person with more brawn than brains who has no regard for what he has given away. The story is presented as if Esau got what he deserved. Jacob is revealed as a heartless schemer who is willing to take advantage of Esau's shortcomings for his own profit. He also shows his cunning in making his brother give up his birthright.

Jacob also schemes to receive Isaac's blessing when Isaac is old, almost blind, and ready to set his house in order. Isaac intends to give his blessing to Esau, his firstborn and favorite son. The blessing of a dying man to his son was considered particularly valuable. It was a blessing that could be given only once: in the world of the Old Testament, when a blessing or a curse had been spoken, it could not be recalled.

With the help of his mother, Rebekah, Jacob deceives Isaac into thinking he is Esau. Convinced that he has Esau before him, the blind Isaac gives his final blessing to Jacob.

The blessing that Jacob receives is for his people, who will one day be the people of Israel. Isaac prays for agricultural prosperity for the Israelites and promises an abundance of wheat and wine. He predicts political success, with countries bowing down before Israel. Finally, Jacob, although the younger, is to rule over the rest of the family.

The biblical writers make it clear that God works mysteriously in this story of intrigue and deception. For God's own reasons,

Jacob was chosen to carry on Isaac's legacy. Jacob was not any worthier than Esau. In important respects, he was less worthy. But he was God's choice.

There is a saying in Christian history that "God writes straight with crooked lines." As we see in the honest portrayal of Jacob and Esau, God accepts people where they are and then calls them to move beyond their faults and limitations to know and serve him and to live fulfilled lives.

14

Jacob's Vision of God
READ GENESIS 28:10–22

Then Jacob woke from his sleep and said,
"Surely the LORD is in this place—and I did not know it!"
GENESIS 28:16

Jacob has a hard life even though he is the one chosen by God. After cheating Esau out of Isaac's final blessing, Jacob has to leave his home, as Esau threatens to kill him. Jacob will never see his parents again. Isaac blesses Jacob once again and tells him to go to his uncle Laban so that Jacob can marry one of his daughters. This is to protect the faith and the family connection to the land promised to Abraham.

While on his journey, Jacob arrives at a certain place and rests there, using a stone for a pillow. In a dream, he receives a divine revelation. He sees a ladder, or perhaps a ramp, going up from earth to heaven. The shape of Jacob's vision may have been inspired by the shape of the ziggurats of Babylon, which had ramps going up their sides to the place where the deity was said to dwell. On the ramp in Jacob's dream are angels, roaming up and down, patrolling the earth and reporting back to God. In his vision, Jacob meets God. God confirms the covenant made to Abraham and to Isaac that their ancestors will be as plentiful as the dust on the ground and will spread from east to west. Jacob will also receive God's protection wherever he goes.

Jacob awakes from the dream shaken by the experience. He recognizes that he has been in the presence of God. He sees the place where he slept as a "gate of heaven" (Genesis 28:17), where messengers of God communicate with the human family and where messages are brought from earth to heaven. Jacob takes the rock that he slept on, puts it on top of a pillar, and dedicates the place to God, calling it Bethel ("house of God"). At this shrine, he pledges himself to the God of his fathers.

Jacob was changed by this experience. He had met the God of promises, who renewed his pledge through Jacob to Abraham's descendants. Jacob in turn made a commitment and promises to God. Since God kept his promises, Jacob must become a man who keeps his promises in return.

This covenant of God through Jacob to the Hebrew people shows a difference between the Hebrews' experience of God and that of their neighbors. The neighboring peoples believed that the gods were territorial and limited in their influence to the borders of the country or city in which they resided. The God of Abraham, Isaac, and Jacob was not limited to any geographical setting but accompanied worshipers wherever they went.

About: Leah, Rachel, and the Twelve Tribes of Israel

The story of Jacob continues in Genesis 29. Jacob arrives in Haran, the home of his uncle Laban, where he meets Rachel, one of Laban's daughters, and immediately falls in love. Laban agrees that Jacob should marry her but first requires Jacob to give him seven years of labor.

At the end of the seven years, Laban agrees to fulfill his commitment. Jacob marries the heavily veiled bride and takes her to the marriage bed, only to discover the next morning that he has married Leah, the older daughter of Laban. Jacob the schemer has been tricked.

When Jacob confronts Laban, Laban tells him that it is the custom for the older daughter to marry before the younger. He then proposes that Jacob can marry Rachel in return for another seven years of service. Jacob accepts the proposal and one week later marries Rachel. (Marriage to more than one wife was common in this society.) Leah and Rachel have no voice in the matter. Leah knows that Jacob does not love her but loves Rachel. Rachel loves Jacob. The two sisters struggle for Jacob's favor. Leah knows she will never match Rachel for Jacob's affections, so she prays for children to show her superiority.

Leah has four sons and gives them names with meanings that show her misery as an unloved wife: Reuben ("the Lord has looked on my affliction"), Simeon ("the Lord has heard that I am hated"), Levi ("my husband will be joined to me"), and

Judah ("I will praise the Lord"). Rachel has no children, so she gives her maidservant Bilhah to Jacob. Bilhah bears two sons in Rachel's name: Dan ("God has judged me and has also heard my voice") and Naphtali ("I have wrestled with my sister and have prevailed"). Leah also gives her maidservant to Jacob, and Zilpah bears two sons: Gad ("good fortune!") and Asher ("women will call me happy"). Leah has two more sons of her own: Issachar ("God has given me my hire") and Zebulun ("my husband will honor me"). Leah also has a daughter, Dinah ("justice").

Rachel finally has a son, Joseph ("may the Lord add to me another son"), and then another, Benjamin ("son of the right hand"). Rachel dies giving birth to Benjamin.

These two wives of Jacob and their maidservants Bilhah and Zilpah gave birth to the founders of the twelve tribes of Israel. The women were seen as blessed by future mothers of the Hebrew people: "May the Lord make the woman who is coming into your house like Rachel and Leah, who together built up the house of Israel. May you produce children in Ephrathah and bestow a name in Bethlehem" (Ruth 4:11).

15

Jacob Returns to the Land of His Fathers

READ GENESIS 31–33

But Esau ran to meet him, and embraced him.

GENESIS 33:4

After the second seven years of service to Laban is finished, Jacob continues to work for his father-in-law. In this arrangement, Jacob is not paid but is able to increase his own herds of sheep and goats at the expense of Laban. In light of Jacob's success, Laban grows jealous. Jacob hears the call to return to his father's land, a decision that Leah and Rachel support. Jacob, his wives, and their servants leave as quickly as they can. Laban chases them for a while, but eventually he reaches an agreement with Jacob in which each will stay in his own land and no longer have a relationship with the other.

Jacob now has to face Esau, the brother whom he has cheated out of every important blessing. Jacob is naturally nervous about the reception he will receive. He divides his family and his herds and sends them in different directions. If Esau attacks him, one half of Jacob's herds and family might be destroyed, but the other could escape safely. He also sends Esau a present of goats, ewes, rams, camels, colts, cows, bulls, and donkeys. Jacob hopes that this will be enough to appease Esau.

That night Jacob wrestles with a man who he realizes is a messenger from God. The man has trouble winning the match, so he touches Jacob's hip, dislocating it. The man then blesses Jacob and tells him that his name is now Israel, because he wrestled with God and prevailed.

The next morning, Jacob goes out to meet Esau, who has come with four hundred men. Jacob walks forward, leading Leah, Rachel, and their children, and bows down seven times as he approaches his brother. But "Esau ran to meet him, and embraced him, and fell on his neck and kissed him, and they wept" (Genesis 33:4).

Esau at first declines the gifts that Jacob has offered, but Jacob prevails on him to accept them, as God has provided Jacob with all that he needs. Esau then accepts the gifts. The brothers depart in peace.

Esau is usually remembered only as the victim of Jacob's schemes. He is seldom remembered for his generosity of spirit when he met Jacob returning home, when he reached out in tears to be reconciled with his brother.

16

Joseph and His Brothers
READ GENESIS 37

They said to one another, "Here comes this dreamer."
GENESIS 37:19

The tale of Joseph and his brothers is one of the vivid stories of the Old Testament. In this story (told in Genesis 37–50), we see how Joseph grows into a model of what it means to live in personal relationship with God. Joseph was self-disciplined and knew how to act in a variety of social situations. He knew when to speak and what to say. Above all, he was aware of God's presence through all of his difficulties.

As Rachel's first child, Joseph is Jacob's favorite. Jacob shows his love by having a long robe with sleeves made for Joseph (it was not many colored). Joseph's brothers are furious over this favoritism shown to him. They will not speak to him and avoid his company.

Joseph does not help matters when he tells his brothers of his dreams. In his dreams he sees them all binding sheaves of wheat in the fields, with his sheaf standing up and the sheaves of his brothers bowing down to it. He tells them of a dream in which the sun, the moon, and eleven stars bow down before him. Joseph does not brag about these dreams but reflects on their possible meaning. His brothers hate him even more.

The brothers are tending to Jacob's sheep at a distance from the main camp when Jacob sends Joseph out to them. The brothers see him coming, recognizing his special cloak. They decide to kill him. But Rueben, the eldest, convinces the rest of the brothers that killing Joseph would be a bad idea, so they put him in a dry well. As the brothers sit by the well eating a meal, a caravan of Ishmaelite traders passes by on its way to Egypt. Seizing the opportunity to earn some cash, the brothers sell Joseph into slavery.

Now the brothers must tell Jacob what happened to Joseph. So they kill a goat and soak Joseph's cloak in its blood. They bring the bloody cloak to Jacob, saying that they discovered it on the road. Believing their story, Jacob mourns his loss. He has been tricked, just as he tricked his own father.

Joseph is now on his way to Egypt. A victim of his brothers' evil intentions, Joseph is an example of how God can use evil to bring about good results. Evil behavior may for a time frustrate God's designs, but in the long run it cannot stop what God intends.

About: Egypt in the
Time of the Patriarchs

T he story of Joseph tells how the Hebrew people came from a life among herders and shepherds to the settled life of Egypt. When Joseph arrived, the pyramids were already ancient. Egypt was a long, thin country split in two by the Nile River as it flowed northward out of Africa. A self-sufficient world located in a narrow river valley, Egypt was surrounded by dry, hot, and unwelcoming deserts. Most Egyptians were farmers living on a twelve-mile-wide strip of land on either side of the Nile. Isolated from the rest of the Near East, Egypt developed a distinctive and rich society.

Egypt was called "the gift of the Nile." Each year the river rose from the floods caused by the melting snows in Kenya. The floods covered the land, and when the waters receded, a new layer of fertile silt was left behind. With its warm climate and fertile lands, Egypt developed a rich agricultural economy. Egypt produced wheat, barley, and a variety of vegetables and fruits. Surrounding countries were dependent on Egypt for food, especially in times of famine.

The rhythm of the rising and receding waters meant that there were basically two seasons in Egypt—the farming season, when the workers would be in the fields cultivating their crops, and the flood season, when they waited for the waters to recede. During the flood season, pharaohs used the people to build the Sphinx and the huge sanctuaries for the dead like the pyramids.

Joseph probably came to Egypt in the period between 1756 BC and 1526 BC. In this period, invaders called the Hyksos, or "rulers of foreign lands," attacked Egypt with their superior military technology. They gained control of the Egyptian delta and most of the northern portion of the Nile Valley. They took upon themselves the trappings of the Egyptian monarchy and aristocracy.

The Hyksos were Semites, similar to Jacob and his family. In this political climate, young and bright Semites like Joseph could advance to positions of power. This also was a period of social and economic commerce between Syria, Canaan, and Egypt, as reflected in the story of Abraham visiting Egypt and the story of Joseph entering Egypt as a slave.

17

Joseph and Pharaoh
READ GENESIS 39–41

*And Pharaoh said to Joseph, "See,
I have set you over all the land of Egypt."*
GENESIS 41:41

Joseph is sold to Potiphar, an Egyptian official. Joseph impresses Potiphar with his abilities and is made overseer of Potiphar's household. But Potiphar's wife falsely accuses Joseph of dishonoring her, and Joseph is thrown into prison. While there, Joseph impresses the jailer, who makes him responsible for all of the prisoners. He meets Pharaoh's cupbearer and household baker—two men who have fallen further than he.

Pharaoh was ruler of Egypt, and the positions of cupbearer and baker were given to the most trusted men in his household. They were the men responsible for preparing Pharaoh's food and drink and protecting him from being poisoned. Now they had lost favor with Pharaoh.

Both men are having strange dreams. They are troubled by the dreams but have no one to interpret them. Joseph tells them to tell him their dreams; he will interpret them with God's help. Joseph tells the cupbearer that he will return to Pharaoh's favor and the baker that he will be executed in three days. When Joseph proves to be right, he asks the cupbearer to remember him when he returns to Pharaoh's court. The cupbearer forgets, and Joseph remains in prison.

Two years after the cupbearer returns to court, Pharaoh is having troubling dreams. He dreams of seven fat cows being eaten by seven lean cows and seven plump, ripened stalks of grain being eaten by seven withered stalks. When no one can interpret these dreams, the cupbearer finally remembers his promise to Joseph.

Pharaoh has Joseph brought before him. Joseph hears the dreams and correctly interprets their meaning. The seven fat cows and stalks of grain are seven years in which harvests will be abundant and the cows will be fat. The next seven years will be a period of famine. After interpreting the dreams, Joseph advises that Pharaoh appoint someone to oversee the harvesting and ensure that enough grain is saved in the first seven years to help Egypt survive the seven years of famine. Pharaoh agrees and appoints Joseph vizier, second in authority only to Pharaoh himself, to carry out the plan. Joseph marries an Egyptian woman and has two sons. The first he names Manasseh ("forgotten"), to show that his previous suffering has been forgotten. The second is Ephraim ("God has made me fruitful").

Joseph had survived and prospered. But he did not take any personal credit for his success. Joseph recognized that God was always with him in the midst of his difficulties, and he celebrated God's goodness in his success.

18

Joseph and His Brothers Are Reconciled

READ GENESIS 42–45

He said, "I am your brother, Joseph,
whom you sold into Egypt."
GENESIS 45:4

Jacob's family in Canaan suffers from the famine predicted by Joseph. Jacob sends ten of Joseph's brothers to Egypt to buy grain. Having lost Joseph, he does not want to lose his youngest son, Benjamin, so he keeps him home.

Arriving in Egypt, the brothers come before Joseph. They see a powerful, shaven, and regal official whom they do not recognize. But Joseph recognizes his brothers and decides to test them. He accuses the brothers of spying and has them questioned. Joseph keeps them in jail for three days, finally releasing them and giving them the grain they purchased. Joseph keeps Simeon as a hostage and tells the brothers to bring the youngest brother, Benjamin, should they return. The brothers are puzzled by Joseph's behavior, especially when they discover that their money has been given back to them.

When the brothers arrive home, they tell Jacob that they have to take Benjamin with them when they return to Egypt. Jacob, horrified, resists. After the family has eaten all the grain, the brothers know they must return to Egypt with Benjamin. Jacob reluctantly but finally agrees. Back in Egypt, the brothers discover that Joseph is still in charge. He gives them a banquet and is so moved by the sight of Benjamin that he leaves the room.

The brothers leave with more grain, only this time Joseph has his own silver cup placed in Benjamin's bag. The brothers are stopped by Joseph's chief steward, who accuses them of theft. When the cup is found in Benjamin's bag, he is accused of stealing it. Joseph tells the brothers that Benjamin will become his slave.

In reply, the brothers admit that they have committed a crime, but it is not the stealing of the cup—it is having sold Joseph into slavery. They now have to face God's judgment for this. They stress Jacob's grief at the loss of Joseph. He could not face the loss of Benjamin. Joseph's brother Judah offers himself as a substitute for Benjamin.

From this, Joseph learns that the brothers have repented and realizes that he must reveal himself: "Then Joseph could no longer control himself before all those who stood by him, and he cried out, 'Send everyone away from me.' So no one stayed with him when Joseph made himself known to his brothers. And he wept so loudly that the Egyptians heard it, and the household of Pharaoh heard it. Joseph said to his brothers, 'I am Joseph. Is my father still alive?'" (Genesis 45:1–3).

Joseph tells his stunned brothers not to feel guilty. God sent him to Egypt to prepare the way for them. The brothers return to Canaan and tell the astonished Jacob of Joseph. Jacob then brings the rest of the family to Egypt and embraces his son.

CCC, 312–14: Providence and the scandal of evil

About: From Joseph to Moses

The story of Joseph recounts the memory of the Hebrew people coming to Egypt. After the time of Joseph, the Hebrews lived in Egypt in apparent peace and prosperity for hundreds of years. We have no record of their accomplishments or stories during this time. The Old Testament picks up the tale of the Hebrews at about 1300 BC, when they were suffering under different Egyptian rulers than those who had welcomed them.

The period of the Hyksos's control ended when Egyptian armies from the south defeated the Hyksos rulers in the mid-1500s BC. Native Egyptian pharaohs again ruled the land. Two of the important pharaohs of this period are Seti I and his son Ramses II. They moved the Egyptian capital north from the city of Thebes, in the southern part of the Nile Valley, to the delta region bordering the Sinai Desert. There they built new cities using slave labor. Scholars believe that the cities of Pithom and Rameses, mentioned in Exodus 1:11, were built in this period.

Losing the political patronage they had under the Hyksos, the Hebrews became slaves.

They were delivered from slavery under the leadership of Moses, the most important figure of the Old Testament. Moses is the principal character in the books of Exodus, Leviticus, Numbers, and Deuteronomy. He is described in unequaled terms: "Never since has there arisen a prophet in Israel like Moses, whom the LORD knew face to face" (Deuteronomy 34:10).

Born of Hebrew parents and raised by Pharaoh's daughter, Moses escaped from Egypt after he killed an Egyptian who was beating a Hebrew slave. Called by God to bring the message of salvation to the Hebrews, Moses succeeded with God's help and brought the people to Mount Sinai to hear the Law.

Moses was responsible for bringing God's Law to the people, organizing their religious life, and intervening with God on their behalf. After years of wandering, fighting, and complaining, the people finally entered the Promised Land, but Moses saw them enter without him. The book of Deuteronomy is a long sermon presented as Moses' farewell address.

In the memory of Israel, Moses was the ideal judge and administrator of the Law. He was the model prophet and intercessor with God and the founder of the life of worship. In later traditions, the first five books of the Bible are called the "Book of Moses."

Moses is given similar respect in the New Testament, where there are repeated appeals to what Moses said (see Matthew 8:4; Matthew 19:7; Matthew 22:24; Mark 7:10; John 7:22; Romans 10:5). In Matthew's Gospel especially, the life and teachings of Jesus are modeled after the life and teachings of Moses. Although Jesus is presented as "greater than Moses" (see Hebrews 3:3), there is no question of Jesus' immense respect for his great predecessor.

CCC, 62; 72: God forms his people Israel;
219: God's love; 581: Jesus and the Law

19

The Birth of Moses

READ EXODUS 1–2

She named him Moses, "because," she said,
"I drew him out of the water."
EXODUS 2:10

The yearly flooding of the Nile River and the precious silt it left behind were a gift of life. Pharaoh abused that gift when he ordered that all Hebrew baby boys be drowned in the Nile. Ironically, Moses, the liberator of Israel, would be saved by this instrument of death.

When we discuss a great figure like Moses, we too often forget the courageous decisions of ordinary people who made that person's life possible. In the case of Moses, his mother, Jochebed; his sister, Miriam; and one of Pharaoh's daughters were the reason he survived.

The Hebrew woman Jochebed has a son. Instead of giving him up to be killed, she sees how good he is and hides him from the Egyptians. When it is impossible to hide him any longer, she fashions a basket, covering it with pitch (as Noah did with the ark to save life on earth), and places it in the river.

The baby boy's sister, Miriam, keeps an eye on the basket and watches while Pharaoh's daughter discovers it. Pharaoh's daughter has pity on the baby boy, draws him out of the water, and names him Moses. Miriam proposes that Jochebed become Moses' nurse, and Pharaoh's daughter agrees. When he is weaned, Moses is brought to Pharaoh's daughter and is raised as her son.

Jochebed is a major figure in the Bible. She looks on Moses and calls him "good," just as God looked at creation and found it good (Genesis 1:4, 10, 12, 18, 21, 25). She saves Moses by preparing a tiny ark covered with pitch for him and placing him in the water. In the same way, human and animal life was saved in the ark of salvation built by Noah. Using these images, the writer is telling us that Jochebed was a source of life for the people in the manner of God and her ancestors.

Moses' sister, Miriam, is the link between Moses' mother and Pharaoh's daughter. She linked the woman of Egypt and the woman of Israel in the act of saving Moses. Through her brave actions, Moses was restored to his mother.

Pharaoh's daughter completes the circle. She knew of her father's decree. She realized that Moses would be drowned if he was found by other Egyptians, as he was clearly Hebrew. Seeing Moses and moved to pity, she defied her father's command. She would not be oppressed by an unjust law, and by her actions she broke the cycle of violence that would have killed Moses.

CCC, 2270–75: Sacredness of human life

20

Moses Meets God in the Burning Bush
READ EXODUS 3

God said to Moses, "I AM WHO I AM."
EXODUS 3:14

In Egypt, the slavery of the Hebrews continues. God hears their groaning and remembers the covenant he made with Abraham, Isaac, and Jacob. In the Old Testament, "to remember" means to bring what is remembered into the present and to act upon it. In remembering, God hears the cries of the poor and takes action.

By this time, Moses has left Egypt, having fled for his life after killing an Egyptian. Making his way to Midian, Moses becomes part of the family of Jethro, marrying his daughter Zipporah. While out tending Jethro's sheep, Moses is captivated by a burning bush that is not consumed in the fire. Approaching the bush, Moses realizes he is in the presence of God.

From the bush, God identifies himself as the God of Abraham, Isaac, and Jacob. God calls on Moses to remember with him the oppression of the Hebrews. God is sending Moses to bring them to freedom. Moses, astonished, asks God for his name. To ask for a person's name in the ancient world was an attempt to gain access to a person's energy and potential. People called on the names of their gods in order to tap into their power.

God answers Moses, "I AM WHO I AM" (Yahweh). Other meanings of God's answer can be "I come to be all that exists" and "I cause to be all that happens." God seems to be saying that God will come in his own time and will not be controlled by Moses. God will be who he will be. He came to save the people because it is his choice. "And he said, 'I will make all my goodness pass before you, and will proclaim before you the name, "The LORD"; and I will be gracious to whom I will be gracious, and will show mercy on whom I will show mercy'" (Exodus 33:19).

To carry out his plan, God chooses Moses. Moses, obviously frightened, objects that he has neither the talent nor the importance to carry out such a task. In a dialogue that finds Moses hesitant and God patient but insistent, Moses is drafted by God to carry out the plan. God promises that the Hebrews will freely walk away from their oppressors; in fact, they will be asked to go. The God who is has always been present to them. Now God will continue to be present as he calls them to an uncertain future.

CCC, 204–8: God reveals his name

21

Pharaoh's Contest with God

READ EXODUS 5–6

*Moses and Aaron went to Pharaoh and said, "Thus says the
LORD, the God of Israel, 'Let my people go.'"*
EXODUS 5:1

Moses returns to Egypt. Accompanied by his brother,
Aaron, he goes to Pharaoh. Moses requests that the
Hebrews be allowed a three-day journey into the desert to
celebrate a religious festival. Pharaoh immediately rejects
the request. He then acts to discredit Moses. He orders the
Hebrews to make their allotted number of bricks but does not
give them the straw they need, so they have to gather straw at
night to make the required number. The people are naturally
upset with Moses and Aaron, and Moses is troubled that he has
only brought more misery upon the people.

But Moses does not quit. Now the battle becomes one
between God and the forces of Egypt, symbolized by Pharaoh.
This dramatic contest is related in Exodus 5–10. Pharaoh's
stubbornness brings ever more severe suffering for his people.
The plagues can be seen as coming in sets of three, each set
ending with an unannounced plague. In the first set, God and

Moses mobilize blood, frogs, and gnats. The second set brings flies, pestilence, and fever boils upon the Egyptians. Finally, the Egyptians suffer hail, locusts, and darkness.

God has Moses warn Pharaoh of the consequence of his actions before all but the third, sixth, and ninth plagues. In those three, God acts without warning. The intent of the plagues is to show the superiority of God's messengers (Exodus 7:17; 8:10; 9:13) and God's continuing presence among his people as they are protected from the plagues (Exodus 8:22; 9:4, 6). God's supremacy is indicated in Exodus 9:14: "I will send all my plagues upon you . . . so that you [Pharaoh] may know that there is no one like me in all the earth." The plagues are not only warnings to Pharaoh, but also a demonstration of God's power for the sake of his people.

When we think of the plagues, it is easy to think in two extremes. On the one hand, our familiarity with the spectacular images created by Hollywood special effects can lead us to see the plagues as illusions. On the other hand, many scholars try to find natural explanations for what is described in the Bible. Both ways of thinking are foreign to the intent of the writer of the text. The biblical writer emphasizes the astounding nature of the events and their onetime character. The writer wanted to emphasize God's work through the powers of nature in order to reveal his supreme power on behalf of the Hebrews.

Despite the plagues on his people, Pharaoh still ignores God. This sets the stage for the final, disastrous plague.

About: Election in the Old Testament

The theme of election, of God choosing a people to be his special possession (Exodus 19:5), is at the heart of the Bible. The choice of a people was God's alone; the people themselves did not merit their choice: "It was not because you were more numerous than any other people that the LORD set his heart on you and chose you—for you were the fewest of all peoples" (Deuteronomy 7:7).

Why God chose this particular people is a mystery: "Although heaven and the heaven of heavens belong to the LORD your God, the earth with all that is in it, yet the LORD set his heart in love on your ancestors alone and chose you, their descendants after them, out of all the peoples, as it is today" (Deuteronomy 10:14–15).

God set the people free from Egypt. The relationship between God and the people was sealed in the covenant on Mount Sinai (Exodus 20:1–19). "Keep his statutes and his commandments, which I am commanding you today for your own well-being and that of your descendants after you, so that you may long remain in the land that the LORD your God is giving you for all time" (Deuteronomy 4:40).

But the people did not always follow the laws that God commanded. The prophets made it clear that if the people lost their sense of God's priorities, God could withdraw his protection: "You only have I known of all the families of the earth; therefore I will punish you for all your iniquities" (Amos 3:2).

Suffering followed—the destruction of Israel and Judah—and in the soul-searching that the people had to do, they recognized that to be God's chosen people was not to be set apart from the world for the sake of prosperity. Rather, it was to be a sign of God's care for the entire world. "I am the LORD, I have called you in righteousness, I have taken you by the hand and kept you; I have given you as a covenant to the people, a light to the nations" (Isaiah 42:6).

> *CCC*, 761–62: The church—prepared for
> in the old covenant

22

Passover

READ EXODUS 11–13

Take your flocks and your herds, as you said, and be gone.
EXODUS 12:32

The contest between Pharaoh and God comes to a lethal climax. As the plagues increase, Pharaoh waffles between letting the people go and keeping them in slavery. The text describes God as hardening Pharaoh's heart. Here the writer is emphasizing that everything that happened was under God's control. Pharaoh's heart was hardened as a result of his own stubbornness in not giving the people freedom and ignoring God's commands.

In Exodus 11, God tells Moses that there will be a final plague. The firstborn of the Egyptians will die at midnight. Moses warns Pharaoh that weeping and wailing will fill Egypt as the result of Pharaoh's decision. Pharaoh is still determined to keep his slaves. Moses leaves angry at Pharaoh's stubbornness.

Moses gathers the people. He orders that a lamb be sacrificed and the blood of the lamb be put on the doorframes of the houses. This will be a sign to God to "pass over" the houses of the Hebrews. That night the Hebrews eat roasted lamb and unleavened bread, preparing for the journey. Egyptian houses are filled with mourning, "for there was not a house without someone dead" (Exodus 12:30). Pharaoh, finally convinced that he cannot defeat God, lets the people go.

The Passover meal probably had its origins in the practice of shepherds sacrificing a spring lamb to ensure the safety and fertility of their flocks. This was combined with a festival practiced in agricultural societies in which the first fruits of the grain harvest were offered. The grain, ground into flour, was not mixed with yeast to emphasize its purity. The genius of the Hebrew writer was to take these two festivals and reinterpret them as celebrations of God's action in history. As the people celebrated these festivals, they remembered the saving action of God in freeing them from Egypt. In Exodus 12, we see the development of Passover laws so that this event would never be forgotten.

The Passover is still remembered by the Jewish people today as a feast of redemption. When the people reenact the ritual and tell the story, the power of the event is made present today, and the people commit themselves once again to God. In the Passover celebration, the youngest member asks about the Passover story. The leader explains that in remembering the events of the past, and in telling the story, we are the people who are protected by the blood of the lamb, who begin the Exodus journey, and who will be protected while crossing the desert.

> *CCC*, 1080–82; 1096: The liturgy;
> 1150–52: Signs and symbols

23

Journey to the Sea
READ EXODUS 14:1–15:21

The waters returned and covered the chariots and the chariot drivers, the entire army of Pharaoh.

EXODUS 14:28

Pharaoh has lost the battle with God. The deaths of the firstborn in Egypt finally made him realize that he was fighting a God who was too strong for him, so he let the Hebrews go. It is impossible to determine the exact date of the Hebrews' departure. Exodus 12:40–42 states that they had been in Egypt for 430 years. If they had come to Egypt during the time when the Hyksos entered Egypt, around 1720, then the date of the Exodus would be about 1290 BC.

Under God's guidance, the people do not take the shortest route to Canaan, as there are military posts along the way. The Hebrews travel south to the Sea of Reeds (mistranslated as Red Sea). Scholars believe that this was a marshy area south of Suez where it was possible to cross the Nile River in the dry season. On the journey, the Hebrew people are led by a pillar of cloud by day and a pillar of fire by night, signifying God's continuing presence.

After letting the Hebrews go, Pharaoh, as was his habit, has a change of heart. He realizes that without the Hebrews, his building projects will suffer for lack of workers. Pharaoh calls out his army, and with six hundred of his finest chariots, they pursue the Hebrews.

Seeing the advancing Egyptian army, the people are terrified. They accuse Moses of leading them into the wilderness to die. Moses appeals for calm. The battle between God and Pharaoh, representing the Egyptian gods, reaches its final climax. God orders Moses to stretch out his arm over the sea: "Then Moses stretched out his hand over the sea. The LORD drove the sea back by a strong east wind all night, and turned the sea into dry land; and the waters were divided. The Israelites went into the sea on dry ground, the waters forming a wall for them on their right and on their left" (Exodus 14:21–22).

Following Moses, and believing in God, the Hebrews reach the other side of the sea. As the Egyptians attempt to follow, Moses stretches out his arm, and the waters flow once again. The Egyptian army is swallowed up, securing God's victory.

Beyond all reason, a people who had little hope against a powerful civilization have been given their freedom. They respond by singing songs of praise to God for his goodness and for his mighty hand in securing their release.

CCC, 1094: The harmony of the Old and
New Testaments; 1221–23: Baptism prefigured

24

Testing in the Desert

READ EXODUS 15:22–17:16

Moses said to them, "It is the bread that
the LORD has given you to eat."
EXODUS 16:15

The Hebrew people began their journey with excitement and anticipation, but they soon discover that the road to freedom is difficult. They are tempted to go back to the safety of the life they knew in slavery, to the leeks and onions that flavored their meals in Egypt. The Hebrew people enter into a time of testing. Altogether, God will test the people or the people will test God ten times in the desert wanderings.

The first test is in the wilderness of Shur. The people arrive at a place called "bitterness." This referred to the water they are unable to drink. They fear for their lives and complain to Moses and God. Moses cries out to God. God tells him how to make the water sweet. This first test was to see if the people would rely on God alone.

The journey continues, and as the Hebrew people move more deeply into the wilderness, the food shortage becomes more severe. The people complain. Again, the life of a slave in Egypt seems more attractive. Will God provide?

God sends bread from heaven, manna, and gives specific instructions on how it is to be gathered and stored. Quail also appears, covering the camp and providing enough food for the day.

Manna is the honeylike secretion of two kinds of scale insects who live in the tamarisk tree and feed on its sap. The sap is rich in carbohydrates but poor in nitrogen. The insects feed on vast quantities of the sap to get nitrogen and secrete the excess sap as honeydew. The honeydew is rich in three kinds of sugar and pectin. Evaporating in the dry desert air, it is found as sticky droplets on plants on the ground. Manna continues to be harvested by the people of the desert today in late May and early June, as it was in the Exodus story.

The people are to gather only enough manna for the day and not to stockpile it. This will show their willingness to depend on God alone. Those who do not have faith that God will provide for tomorrow discover that their stockpiled manna has melted away.

The Hebrew people considered the appearance of the quail and the manna to be a miracle. It was not a miracle in the sense that something magical happened, but in the sense that the food they needed to continue the journey appeared when they needed it. As they continue their journey, they begin to realize that their riches are in God alone.

CCC, 1094: The harmony of the Old and New
Testaments; 1334: Signs of bread and wine

About: Miriam

We are first introduced to Moses' sister, Miriam, in the story of Moses' birth. Miriam followed Moses' basket down the river and saw Pharaoh's daughter draw him out. She arranged for Moses' mother to act as nursemaid. Because of her watchfulness and courage, Moses was restored to his mother.

Miriam was also a prophet. When Moses led the triumphant song praising God for the victory over the Egyptians at the Sea of Reeds, Miriam provided the refrain: "Then the prophet Miriam, Aaron's sister, took a tambourine in her hand; and all the women went out after her with tambourines and with dancing. And Miriam sang to them: 'Sing to the LORD, for he has triumphed gloriously; horse and rider he has thrown into the sea'" (Exodus 15:20–21).

As a prophet, Miriam was a messenger for God. As a witness for God, Miriam shared with Moses and Aaron the call to stir the imagination of the people so that they could see a better future. God had saved the Hebrews from the static gods of Egypt who would have kept them in slavery and led them to victory over slavery and death. Moses' song with Miriam's refrain not only praised God for saving the people, but also described the brilliant future in the land that the Lord had promised to them (Exodus 15:1–21).

In the book of Numbers, Miriam appears with Aaron to challenge Moses' leadership. They accuse Moses of marrying a foreign woman and challenge his authority as God's principal spokesman. Moses, described as the humblest of men, brings them into the meeting tent. There God speaks to Aaron and

Miriam. God makes it clear that while he may speak to the prophets in a number of ways, he speaks to Moses face-to-face.

Miriam turns snow-white, like a person who has leprosy. Aaron pleads to Moses to intercede for Miriam. Moses prays for her healing. Following the law concerning those recovering from skin diseases found in Leviticus 13:4–6, Miriam is confined for seven days. The whole community waits for Miriam to heal and does not move on until she is restored to them.

The deaths of Miriam and Aaron are reported in Numbers 20. Miriam was buried at Kadesh, whose meaning is "sacred," an important sanctuary on Israel's journey in the desert. With Moses and Aaron, Miriam is remembered as one of the great leaders of the Exodus. She was a leader in praising God and a prophet bringing God's word to the people. The people would not move forward without her, and when she died she was buried in a sacred sanctuary.

CCC, 64: Holy women; 2577: Intercession

25

The Hebrews Meet God at Sinai

READ EXODUS 19

Moses brought the people out of the camp to meet God.

EXODUS 19:17

After the escape from the Egyptians, the Hebrew people journey into the wilderness of Sinai, camping in front of Mount Sinai. God calls Moses up to the mountain and reminds him what he has done for the people. "You have seen what I did to the Egyptians, and how I bore you on eagles' wings and brought you to myself" (Exodus 19:4). God promises that the Hebrews will be his "treasured possession" (Exodus 19:5). For God, the Hebrews will be "a priestly kingdom and a holy nation" (Exodus 19:6).

Moses summons the elders and tells them of God's promise. In the name of the people, the elders promise that they will do what God commands of them. Moses brings their answer to God. God promises he will come in a dense cloud so that when the people hear Moses they will trust that he is speaking for God.

The people prepare themselves to meet God. Moses warns them that they will have to be careful not to touch the mountain, as this will mean their death. The people do as Moses commands and wait for God's coming.

Thunder and lightning come on the third day of waiting, along with a thick cloud on the mountain and a loud trumpet blast that makes the people tremble. "Moses brought the people out of the camp to meet God. They took their stand at the foot of the mountain. Now Mount Sinai was wrapped in smoke, because the LORD had descended upon it in fire; the smoke went up like the smoke of a kiln, while the whole mountain shook violently. As the blast of the trumpet grew louder and louder, Moses would speak and God would answer him in thunder" (Exodus 19:17–19).

God calls Moses to the top of the mountain and tells him to bring Aaron up. The rest of the priests are to stay beyond the limits of the mountain, or else they will be punished. When Moses returns with Aaron, Moses learns what God will demand of them in return for the grace of freedom he has given them.

CCC, 62–63: God forms his people Israel;
204: God reveals his name

About: The Sabbath

The pace at which people live in the world today is almost nonstop. We are working longer and harder for less and less. So-called labor-saving devices all too often create more work. While there are many distractions that keep us occupied, there is little that gives a sense of rest.

For the Hebrew people, that sense of rest was provided by the Sabbath, a day when they were not to work. The Hebrew word for Sabbath means "to cease," "to desist," or "to rest." Exodus 20:10–11 says: "But the seventh day is a sabbath to the LORD your God; you shall not do any work—you, your son or your daughter, your male or female slave, your livestock, or the alien resident in your towns. For in six days the LORD made heaven and earth, the sea, and all that is in them, but rested the seventh day; therefore the LORD blessed the sabbath day and consecrated it."

Note who consecrates the Sabbath and what Exodus uses as an example of what it means to rest. Everyone is to rest, even the slaves, the livestock, and the alien who lives in the town. The book of Deuteronomy commands that the slaves are to rest like everyone else, because the Hebrews must remember that they themselves were once slaves (Deuteronomy 5:15). Just as God did not reject the Hebrews but treated them with compassion, they in turn must treat their slaves with compassion.

The Sabbath became especially important when the Jewish people were living in exile in Babylon, without the temple and the other supports for their faith. The observance of the Sabbath as a day of rest and assembly helped the people recognize their distinct vocation as God's people in a strange land.

To ensure a meaningful Sabbath celebration, certain regulations were instituted. The Hebrew people could not gather wood on the Sabbath (Numbers 15:32–36), light fires (Exodus 35:3), prepare food (Exodus 16:23), move from place to place without a good reason (Exodus 16:29), or conduct business activities.

Positively, the Sabbath was a time for praying in community (Leviticus 23:3), offering sacrifice (Numbers 28:9–10), and giving to the priests twelve loaves of unleavened bread as an offering to God (showbread). The fresh bread remained as an offering to God for the week, and the priests ate the old loaves.

The Sabbath united the Jewish people. On this day, they celebrated their unique relationship with God, their compassionate relationship with all in their midst, and their gratitude to God for all he had given them.

> *CCC*, 2042–43: Precepts of the church;
> 2174–88: The Christian Sabbath

26

I Am the Lord Your God

READ EXODUS 20:1–11

You shall have no other gods before me
EXODUS 20:3

Exodus 20 is the key text in the Old Testament. It recounts the giving of the Ten Commandments, the basis of the moral law.

When Moses and Aaron go up on Mount Sinai, God first reminds them of what he has done for them: "I am the LORD your God, who brought you out of the land of Egypt, out of the house of slavery" (Exodus 20:2). He then tells them what they need to do in order to live in relationship with God and one another. We call these instructions the Ten Commandments. The first three commandments tell the people what it means to live in relationship with God.

You shall have no other gods before me.

You shall not make for yourself an idol, whether in the form of anything that is in heaven above, or that is on the earth beneath,

> or that is in the water under the earth. You
> shall not bow down to them or worship them;
> for I the LORD your God am a jealous God,
> punishing children for the iniquity of parents,
> to the third and the fourth generation of those
> who reject me, but showing steadfast love to
> the thousandth generation of those who love
> me and keep my commandments. (Exodus
> 20:3–6)

The use of the word *jealous* to describe God's concern for the people has a long tradition in English translations of the Bible, but it is misleading. It gives the impression that God is envious, begrudging, and spiteful toward those who will not hear him. This is not the meaning of the word translated as "jealous" in the Hebrew text. Catholic scholars believe that the word *impassioned* is a better translation. God's concern for the people is total. God is passionately committed to the people.

The writers of the Old Testament did not use abstract statements to describe the consequences of sin. They used examples that the people would understand. They said that generations of people would be affected by sin. To say that the people will be punished to the third and fourth generation illustrates the nature of sin itself. Sin has social consequences. When sin enters a community, it infects the whole community, from generation to generation. We see the truth of this in the prevalence of child abuse, alcoholism, and drug abuse infecting generation after generation.

But the text also says that the effects of sin are limited. God's grace is promised to the thousandth generation of those who follow him. God's love is infinite, while the power of sin is limited.

The second commandment instructs that God's name, Yahweh, is not to be taken in vain, specifically in courts of law, where the name of God is used to swear to the truth.

The third commandment is to keep holy the Sabbath. Since God rests, people should rest also. Note that the command to rest extends to the whole community, even to the slaves and beasts of burden.

CCC, 2083–2094: Man's duties toward God;
2110–11: Superstition; 2118–22: Irreligion

About: Law in the Old Testament

Rules, regulations, dress codes, discipline—all can be annoying facts of life. The notion of law in our country is that rules are to be obeyed without question, and if you don't want to follow the rules, then you should leave. Our attitude toward the law is basically one of suspicion: we recognize that laws are needed, but we wish it were not so.

When we think of the Old Testament, we too often think of it as a religion of law, as opposed to the New Testament, which shows a religion of love. This is a mistake.

The God of love is not a strange concept in the Old Testament. The Law in the Old Testament is God's gracious guidance for life. Even today in Jewish worship, the Torah is kept in a sacred receptacle and is brought out with singing and dancing.

Psalm 119 gives a loving sense of the importance of the Law for life in Old Testament times. It begins by praising the way of the Law as the way to happiness: "Happy are those whose way is blameless, who walk in the law of the LORD. Happy are those who keep his decrees, who seek him with their whole heart, who also do no wrong, but walk in his ways" (Psalm 119:1–3).

Throughout the psalm the law is mentioned with delight, and the psalmist meditates on and loves the Law because it shows God's continuing concern for his people: "I know, O LORD, that your judgments are right, and that in faithfulness you have humbled me. Let your steadfast love become my comfort according to your promise to your servant" (Psalm 119:75–76).

It is through fidelity to the Law that God will lead the believer through times of trouble. "Trouble and anguish have come upon me, but your commandments are my delight. Your decrees are righteous forever; give me understanding that I may live" (Psalm 119:143–144).

It is in following the Law that the believer will find the way to truth and the way to fulfillment as a human being, which God desires for all who follow him.

CCC, 1950–53: The moral law

27

Loving the Neighbor

READ EXODUS 20:7–21

You shall not murder.
EXODUS 20:13

The first part of God's instructions establishes belief in the one God as the foundation of moral life. God has shown his nature by leading the people to freedom. In return, the Hebrew people are to recognize that in order to live in freedom, they must make God the highest priority in their lives. The second part of God's instructions, the remaining seven commandments, establishes the basic principles of how people should treat one another and live in community.

The fourth commandment tells the people to honor their parents. This is a commandment for all within the community, especially the adults, who are to give their elderly parents the respect they deserve. As parents grow older and become more infirm, the young are not to abandon them but to continue to give them the care they need.

The fifth commandment, against killing, has to do with the unjust killing of another. Israel had a death penalty, one that was strictly monitored and controlled. The commandment establishes the principle of reverence for life, a principle extended by Jesus in Matthew 5:21–26 to include total reconciliation with one's neighbor before one prays to God.

The sixth commandment, prohibiting adultery, in its narrowest sense forbids the violation of the wife of another man. It understands a wife as the property and trust of the man. In the broader sense, the commandment prohibits the violation of the marriage vow, which attacks the basis of community life.

The seventh commandment, against stealing, extends to more than the obvious material things. Material goods are necessary for a dignified human life. The commandment is not a defense of private property as an absolute value, as God says from the beginning that all of creation's goods are to be shared with all. This commandment prohibits taking the things people and communities need in order to live in peace with one another and with God.

The eighth commandment, against giving false evidence, concerns courtroom practice. The court is the place where disputes are resolved, so it must be a place where people can be confident that public witness is reliably described and reported.

The ninth and tenth commandments, concerning coveting, highlight the destructive power of desire. To covet does not mean simply to wish for what another has, but to plot to take it away or to destroy the other's good name through lies and slander.

CCC, 2197–2200: Parents and children; 2258: Life is sacred; 2331–36: Male and female; 2401: You shall not steal; 2464: Telling the truth; 2514–16: Ninth commandment; 2534: Tenth commandment

About: The Book of Leviticus

The main subject matter of Leviticus is ritual, and even those parts of the book that are concerned with morality and social order impose a ritual image on moral requirements. In the book of Leviticus, the temple is seen as the center of holiness in the world, where the presence of God is alive. Within the temple was the tabernacle, and within the tabernacle was the sanctuary, which contained the holy place (where the altar was located) and the Holy of Holies (where the Ark of the Covenant was kept). The court surrounding the tabernacle was holy, but to a lesser degree. Surrounding the court was the camp, where the chosen people lived. This was considered not holy but clean, which means it was fit for holy things. Outside the camp was the wilderness, considered unclean.

Only the high priest could enter the inner sanctum, the holiest place. Priests could enter the tabernacle or ascend to the altar. Only people who were in a clean state could enter the court. Those considered unclean had to leave the camp. The holy was the sphere of God; those who were unclean represented what was opposed to God. In the minds of the people of the Old Testament, the distinction between the holy place and holy people and those who were unclean was a concrete reality. The sanctuary where God was present was the holiest place on earth, where God lived in opposition to everything that was evil.

Leviticus 19–22 describes in detail the ritual practices of the people that set them apart from the world. It identifies the people as a holy people. They belonged to God, not just when they were worshiping in the tabernacle of the temple, but at all times. Holiness was a matter of living their daily lives in faithfulness to God, obeying his commands, and living in a right relationship with one another.

In a sense, John 1:14—"And the Word became flesh and lived among us, and we have seen his glory, the glory as of a father's only son, full of grace and truth"—can be seen as a commentary on Leviticus. The phrase *lived among us* actually reads "pitched his tent" among us, an allusion to the tent that was pitched as a tabernacle when the Hebrew people were traveling. The holiness of God is now present in the person of Jesus and, by grace, in all who believe in him.

28

Into the Wilderness

READ NUMBERS 14

Why is the LORD bringing us into this land to fall by the sword? . . . Would it not be better for us to go back to Egypt?

NUMBERS 14:3

The book of Numbers was edited by temple priests who lived in Babylon during the time when the people of Judah were in exile (597–539 BC). The Hebrew people were facing a new journey to the Holy Land. In editing and revising these memories of a time of testing in the wilderness, the priestly writers were instructing their own generation on what it means to be faithful to God, on the cost of disobedience, and on the promise of new life.

As the Hebrew people prepare to leave Sinai, they wait on God and his blessing. God instructs Moses to have Aaron and the priests bless the people by saying: "The LORD bless you and keep you; the LORD make his face to shine upon you, and be gracious to you; the LORD lift up his countenance upon you, and give you peace" (Numbers 6:24–26).

The sign of God's presence with the Hebrew people is the pillar of cloud overshadowing the tabernacle, the tent in which the Ark of the Covenant is kept. When the cloud covers the tabernacle, the people remain in camp for that day. When the cloud disappears, they travel. In this way the Hebrew people are obedient to God, since it is God who guides the journey and not their own decisions (Numbers 9:15–23).

The triumphant procession that begins the journey all too soon becomes a weary hike through the desert of Sinai. As the day-to-day journey becomes longer, the people begin to grumble against Moses and Aaron. They long for the days of easy answers in Egypt, where they only had to do what they were told. The spirit of rebellion even reaches into Moses' family when Aaron and Miriam challenge him for leadership.

Within sight of the Promised Land, the people completely lose heart. Instead of seeing the land of "milk and honey" as a land of opportunity, they listen to their fears and reject God's promises of aid. Therefore, they wander in the desert for another forty years, until the doubting generation dies and the younger generation, tested in the desert, is ready to move forward.

The journey in the book of Numbers reflects everyone's faith journey. The process of growing in faith can include many experiences of joy, wonder, excitement, and conviction. But when the experience of joy fades and life seems not to have changed, the daily grind can wear on commitments made in periods of joy. Freedom in God means making choices that go against the comfortable habits we develop when we let our fears and desires make our choices for us.

CCC, 2574–77: Moses the intercessor

About: The Book of Deuteronomy

In 622 BC, during the reign of King Josiah, the people of Judah were called to a renewal of the covenant. While cleaning out a temple storeroom, workmen found an ancient manuscript of the Law. After listening to a reading of the manuscript, King Josiah tore his robes as a sign of repentance. The manuscript became the basis of his reforms (see chapter 65). It also became the basis for the book of Deuteronomy and for the theological vision found in the books of the Old Testament from Joshua through 2 Kings.

Deuteronomy is presented as the last will and testament of Moses. As the Hebrews prepare to cross into the Promised Land, Moses calls for a renewal of the covenant made by their ancestors in faith. He presents it as a commitment they need to make today. (The text uses the word *today* more than fifty times.) Moses tells the people that "now" is the hour of choice. God has not simply called parents and grandparents into relationship; God calls us today.

Two passages are especially characteristic of the faith God calls us to today. In Deuteronomy 6:4–5, Moses proclaims: "Hear, O Israel: The LORD is our God, the LORD alone. You shall love the LORD your God with all your heart, and with all your soul, and with all your might."

Moses then tells the people to recite this to their children and to carry the prayer close to their heart.

Moses also tells the Hebrew people that God gave them the dignity of the freedom to choose (Deuteronomy 30:15–20). God placed before them the choice of life or death. Those who follow the Lord and his commandments will be choosing life, while those who choose anything less than God will be choosing death. Moses appeals to them to choose life: "I call heaven and earth to witness against you today that I have set before you life and death, blessings and curses. Choose life so that you and your descendants may live, loving the LORD your God, obeying him, and holding fast to him; for that means life to you and length of days, so that you may live in the land that the LORD swore to give to your ancestors, to Abraham, to Isaac, and to Jacob" (Deuteronomy 30:19–20).

There was no gray area here; the choices were clear. God gives every generation this choice. Choosing life is choosing God. God is our first priority.

Deuteronomy ends with a sensitive portrait of Moses' death and burial. He was permitted to see the land before he died and was buried in an unknown grave cared for by God. Joshua will lead the people into the new land.

CCC, 2574–77: Moses the intercessor

About: The Historical Books

Chapters 29 through 54 in this book tell the story of the people of Israel from the time of their possession of the land up to the division of the kingdom. These readings are drawn from the books of Joshua, Judges, 1 and 2 Samuel, and 1 and 2 Kings, the historical books of the Old Testament known in Jewish tradition as the "former prophets." They are also known as the "Deuteronomic history," because they recount Israel's history from a point of view similar to that of the book of Deuteronomy. The Deuteronomic history teaches a consistent lesson, pointing out Israel's infidelity to the covenant.

The other historical books are Ruth, 1 and 2 Chronicles, Ezra, Nehemiah, Tobit, Judith, Esther, and 1 and 2 Maccabees. Chronicles retells much of the story told in Samuel and Kings from a different point of view. It extols the work of God in Israel's history, gives hope, and roots temple worship in the acts of Moses and David.

29

Rahab and the Fall of Jericho

READ JOSHUA 2; 6

As soon as the people heard the sound of the trumpets, they
raised a great shout, and the wall fell down flat.

JOSHUA 6:20

Women played an important role in the story of the Exodus. The midwives frustrated Pharaoh's desire to destroy the male children of the Hebrews. Moses' mother, his sister, and Pharaoh's daughter saved Moses' life. Now, as the Hebrew people are ready to enter the Promised Land, a woman again has an important role in helping them.

When Joshua's spies enter the city of Jericho, they stay in the house of Rahab, a prostitute whose house is built into the city wall. Rahab has no husband or children and is a self-supporting workingwoman. Her house is an inn, an ideal place for strangers to gather and listen for information.

Rahab has also been listening. She has heard about the Hebrew people camped across the Jordan River. She believes that, with God at their side, they are an irresistible force. Therefore, she acts to protect her life and the lives of her parents, brothers, and sisters. She hides Joshua's spies under a pile of flax and sends the soldiers of Jericho who are pursuing them in the wrong direction.

Rahab's faith and *hesed*, or covenant love, are shown in her actions to protect the spies. Having made a commitment to them, she asks for a commitment in return. She wants them to spare her life and those of her family. The spies agree and give her a scarlet cord to tie on the window of her house as a sign of protection.

Joshua 6:20–25 tells the story of the attack on Jericho. All living creatures are being killed by the attacking Hebrew army. Joshua remembers the promise made to Rahab and sends the two spies to bring out Rahab and her kinfolk. Because of Rahab's faith, she and her family are spared and become part of the Hebrew people.

Rahab heard of their God, practiced the covenant virtues, and expected protection in return. God's response through Joshua was to be faithful to the promise: he spared her life and those of her family.

Rahab is mentioned again in the New Testament. She is one of the women included in Matthew's record of Jesus' ancestry (Matthew 1:5). In the letter to the Hebrews, she is named as an example of faith: "By faith Rahab the prostitute did not perish with those who were disobedient, because she had received the spies in peace" (Hebrews 11:31).

She is also mentioned in the epistle of James as an example of someone whose good works confirm her faith: "Likewise, was not Rahab the prostitute also justified by works when she welcomed the messengers and sent them out by another road?" (James 2:25).

About: Joshua

After Moses, Joshua ("Yahweh has saved") is the most revered figure in the early history of Israel. Perhaps only King David was more important among the leaders in the Old Testament. Joshua first appears as a warrior chosen by Moses to lead the Hebrew attack against the Amalekites (Exodus 17:9–13). Throughout the rest of the book of Exodus, we see Moses training Joshua for leadership. He accompanies Moses to Mount Sinai and serves at the tent of meeting. He is one of the spies sent to scout out the land of Canaan, and while the rest of the people lose heart, he is convinced that God will aid Israel and lead them to victory (Numbers 14:6–9). Because of his faithfulness, Joshua is one of the two members of his generation (with Caleb) to live to enter the Promised Land (Numbers 14:30).

As Moses approaches death, God instructs him to name Joshua as his successor, and he does so right before he dies. "Joshua son of Nun was full of the spirit of wisdom, because Moses had laid his hands on him; and the Israelites obeyed him, doing as the LORD had commanded Moses" (Deuteronomy 34:9).

Joshua was not simply the successor of Moses; he also modeled Moses in every way. He was commissioned on holy ground (Joshua 5:13–15; see Exodus 3:5). He told the people to prepare themselves before they heard God's revelation (Joshua 3:5; see Exodus 19:10–11). He interceded for the people after they had sinned (Joshua 7:5–9; see Exodus 32:11–14), and he mediated the covenant between God and the people (Joshua 24:1–28; see Exodus 24:1–18).

Joshua led the Hebrew people from success to success in conquering the land of Canaan. The biblical writer attributes this to his obedience and faithfulness to God. The Canaanite people were defeated, their cities were destroyed, and the spoils of war were offered to God. Like Moses, Joshua was successful until his death, at the age of 110, the same age of Joseph at his death.

In the book of Joshua, we find the ideal person of faith, a person whose commitment and obedience to God is directly responsible for his accomplishing his mission. We also find the three elements that were essential to the Hebrew people's living faithfully with God. First, they had to obey God by listening not only with their ears but also with their minds and hearts. Second, all idols had to be removed from the land, and the spoils of the holy war had to be offered to God. Finally, they had to renew the covenant with God, confirming their commitment to him to secure the land for the future.

30

Joshua Renews the Covenant
READ JOSHUA 23–24

Hold fast to the LORD your God, as you have done to this day.
JOSHUA 23:8

Joshua gives his farewell address to the Hebrew people in Joshua 23–24. He has seen a great deal in the 110 years of his life. He witnessed the Exodus and survived the forty years in the desert. At an age when most men would be in retirement, Joshua was leading the fight against the Canaanites, making difficult decisions concerning the distribution of land, and punishing those who would not follow the Law. In his farewell address, Joshua repeats two themes: faithfulness to God leads to success, and turning away from God leads to failure.

Joshua begins by emphasizing the people's dependence on God and the Law: "Therefore be very steadfast to observe and do all that is written in the book of the law of Moses, turning aside from it neither to the right nor to the left, so that you may not be mixed with these nations left here among you, or make mention of the names of their gods, or swear by them, or serve them, or bow yourselves down to them, but hold fast to the Lord your God, as you have done to this day" (Joshua 23:6–8).

Joshua follows this advice with a warning of what will happen to the Hebrews if they stray from the path of God by following foreign gods and intermarrying with the local cultures: "If you transgress the covenant of the Lord your God, which he enjoined on you, and go and serve other gods and bow down to them, then the anger of the Lord will be kindled against you, and you shall perish quickly from the good land that he has given to you" (Joshua 23:16).

In chapter 24, Joshua renews his personal commitment to God and calls on the people to do the same. He does so by remembering with them all that God has done for them. Joshua retells the stories of Abraham, of Jacob and Esau, of the time in Egypt, and of the Exodus experience. He also recalls their most recent experience of beginning to possess the Promised Land, in which their success was dependent on the Lord (Joshua 24:16–18).

As Moses did in Deuteronomy, Joshua makes the people's choice clear. Serving the "jealous" God of their fathers (again the word translated "jealous" is better translated "impassioned" or "zealous") will bring them life. Failure to do so will bring them death. The people, represented by the elders, say yes to Joshua and to the Lord.

CCC, 1093–95: The Old Testament in Christian liturgy

About: The Settlement of Canaan

I f we were to read the book of Joshua by itself, we would have the impression that the Hebrew people moved quickly over the land of Canaan and, under Joshua's leadership, swept the Canaanites aside. However, looking at the biblical text more closely, we see that the conquest and assimilation of the Promised Land was a more gradual process. The book of Judges indicates that the settlement of the Promised Land involved an ongoing struggle among the various Hebrew tribes against local enemies and one another.

The book of Joshua tells of a military campaign that destroyed the principal cities of Canaan in a relentless display of force. Reading the text more closely, we see that in places the settlement was peaceful, with the seminomadic Hebrew tribes coming out of the desert, settling the land, and then occupying the cities.

More recently, scholars have proposed that the invasion of Canaan by the Hebrew people was accompanied by a revolt of the indigenous peasants against the local rulers. As the peasants succeeded in dethroning the rulers, they joined with and adopted the faith of the invading Hebrew tribes.

One disturbing element of the warfare in Joshua's time is its merciless character. It was the brutal nature of this fighting that probably influenced Rahab to align herself with the Hebrews.

While the fighting itself seems brutal, the people are depicted as remaining faithful to the Law during the settlement of Canaan. When Jericho was taken, Joshua intended that all the loot be set apart for God. This meant that every animal, every piece of treasure, and every person was the property of God, who was given credit for the victory in battle. The material property was turned over to the temple, and the prisoners were killed. According to Deuteronomy 20, this was the process in effect against the cities of Canaan, but historically there are few examples of this ever happening. The description of the practice in the book of Joshua suggests that the text was intended to show that this was an ideal time under an ideal leader in which the Law was practiced to its fullest.

CCC, 2309–17: War and the use of military force

31

Deborah, Barak, and Jael
READ JUDGES 4–5

So perish all your enemies, O LORD!
JUDGES 5:31

The story of Deborah and Barak is told twice in the book of Judges. In chapter 4, it is told in prose. In chapter 5, it is told in a poem, regarded by scholars as one of the earliest poems in the literature of the Old Testament.

The Hebrew people have once again fallen into sin, abandoning their faith in God. One of the kings in Canaan, Jabin, sends his general, Sisera, to invade them with nine hundred iron chariots. Sisera needs no further prompting, as he has been oppressing the Hebrew people for twenty years.

Deborah is a prophet and a judge. With the invasion of Sisera, she calls on Barak, a local Hebrew general, and orders him to defend the land against Sisera. Barak knows that Deborah holds the power and agrees to go, but only if she will accompany him. She agrees but also tells him that the glory of the victory will not come to him: Sisera will die by the hand of a woman.

In the period of Judges, the Hebrew people were a loose confederation of tribes with no central authority to call them together to fight a common enemy. Deborah, in spite of these handicaps, manages to muster six of the tribes to fight against Sisera. With their aid, Barak and his army are able to defeat Sisera, and peace is established in the land for some forty years.

Defeated on the battlefield, Sisera escapes and manages to get to the tent of a woman called Jael. In Judges 4, Jael offers hospitality to Sisera, gives him milk to drink, prepares a bed for him, and, while he sleeps, drives a tent peg through his head. In the poem in Judges 5, she attacks him while he is awake. In any case, when Barak arrives, Jael shows him the dead Sisera, and Deborah's prophecy is fulfilled.

Jael was considered a heroine for the Hebrew people, as she was the one who helped bring salvation to the people. In Deborah's song (Judges 5), Jael is called "most blessed of women," a title used only for Judith and Mary the mother of Jesus, who also are praised for their part in bringing salvation to Israel.

It can be troubling to read about Jael's violent actions. The idea of offering hospitality and then violating it by murder is offensive. Jael, however, was acting to protect herself and her family. She realized that the Hebrew army would not be far behind, and a woman was helpless in the face of a victorious army (see Judges 5:30).

About: The World of the Judges

The book of Judges takes us into a world similar to that of the Wild West of American history. Judges is a collection of stories of men and women who face great challenges while defending themselves and their people. These are stories of success and failure written with a religious message: all success comes from God, and those who fail do so because they depend on themselves.

The term *judge* has two meanings in the Bible. First, it means what we normally think of as a judge: one who either makes decisions in a court or makes a private judgment. Deborah does this in Judges 4:4–5. The second meaning of *judge* refers to the charismatic leaders raised up by God to deliver the people from oppression. Judges were given the power they needed in times of crisis.

There were a number of crises in the new land, because the Hebrews faced a variety of enemies: tribes like the Midianites and the Amalekites (an enemy we first met in Exodus) and competing states like Moab and Ammon. Most important was the arrival of the Philistines, invaders from the sea who set up coastal trading cities. Philistine control spread north from Gaza to about the present city of Tel Aviv. The Philistines were the most serious enemy of the Hebrew people, lasting from about 1200 BC until their defeat by King David, in 965 BC.

The stories that make up the book of Judges were originally stories about heroes of local tribes. They were gathered by the editors of the Bible and compiled in the book of Judges. They show the embellishment of folktales, as the reputation of the hero grew in the telling (see the story of Samson, chapter 33). The editors of the book of Judges collected and used these stories to show a pattern of how God worked with the Hebrew people.

The stories begin with a description of how the people have sinned, falling into the hands of their enemies. In their distress, they cry out to God, who inspires a judge or a savior to deliver them. The stories end with peace returning to the land with the success of the judge. The basic tales illustrate the teaching that sin leads to punishment, and repentance brings deliverance.

The priestly writers collected the stories in the book of Judges in the period of the Exile (597–539 BC). The Jewish people had lost their land and wondered if God had abandoned them. In telling the stories in Judges, the writers were giving the people reasons to hope that God would once again forgive and deliver them.

32

Gideon's Small Army
READ JUDGES 6–8

Deliver Israel from the hand of Midian;
I hereby commission you.
JUDGES 6:14

The Hebrew people once again forget the Lord. This time it is the Midianites who take advantage of their weakness and carry out a full-scale invasion. The Hebrew people cry out to God. God comes to Gideon.

Gideon, a farmer, is threshing his wheat in a winepress so that he can hide it from the Midianites. When God tells him that he will lead the Hebrew people against their enemies, Gideon ridicules the idea. He tells God that God abandoned the people and does not seem prepared to keep his promises. God is not put off; he gives the task to Gideon and promises that he will be with him. Gideon does not think much of God's choice, as his tribe is among the smallest. God, of course, realizes this. God wants to emphasize that when victory comes, it comes from God. The Hebrew people will never win if they depend on themselves.

Gideon begins to carry out his commission by correcting abuses in worship practiced by his own family. His family has become worshipers of the false god Baal, so Gideon dismantles the altar to Baal and creates a new one for God. Gideon's action upsets his neighbors. His father, Joash, defends him, saying that if Baal is really a god he can take care of himself.

Gideon gathers his army and prepares to fight. But God is not done. In a series of demands, God forces Gideon to send home the majority of the gathered soldiers, until his army is limited to three hundred. In the middle of the night, Gideon brings his troops to battle and uses a trick to panic the Midianite soldiers into thinking that he has arrived with a much larger army. In the confusion that follows, the Midianites flee the battlefield, leaving Gideon to capture the camp.

Gideon then chases down the Midianite kings, capturing and killing them. Here we learn that one of his motives is blood vengeance for the deaths of his brothers at the hands of the Midianites.

The Hebrew people are giddy at Gideon's success, and he is offered the kingship. He refuses the title, saying that God alone rules over the people. Gideon does become a judge, however, and allows himself to be decked out with the trappings of wealth from the loot of the pagan kings. This leads the writer to note that Gideon set a bad example that would lead the Hebrew people to continue to abandon God.

33

Samson the Flawed Hero
READ JUDGES 16

He strained with all his might; and the house fell on the lords
and all the people who were in it.
JUDGES 16:30

We saw previously in the story of Jacob that "God writes straight with crooked lines." This is true for all of us: we are imperfect people who fulfill our calls through God's grace. It is important to think of the depth of God's mercy when we read the story of Samson.

Samson is born after an angel appears to his mother and tells her that she will bear a son who will be consecrated to God. From the time of his birth, Samson is a Nazirite, which means that he is not to drink wine or strong drink, eat anything unclean, or cut his hair. Samson grows into a man of strength, but throughout the story he systematically breaks his Nazirite vows.

Judges 14–16 shows Samson fighting the Philistines for the sake of his tribe, the Danites. Samson is a man of mighty exploits. Many of his adventures are the result of his attraction to beautiful women. The first is his wife, not a woman of Israel, but a Philistine. At his wedding feast, Samson gives the guests a riddle based on his exploit of killing a lion and later eating the honey from a beehive that formed in the lion's skull. He bets linen garments that the guests will not guess the answer. They threaten Samson's wife and her family to get her to tell them the meaning of the riddle. When they answer Samson correctly, he is enraged. He kills thirty men to get their cloaks to pay his debt.

When Samson returns to visit his wife, he discovers that she has been given to another man. In revenge, he sets fire to the grain fields in harvesttime. When he is captured by the Philistines, he destroys one thousand of them with the jawbone of a donkey.

Samson meets his downfall in the beautiful Delilah, who learns from him the secret of his strength. Samson's long hair symbolizes the strength of fidelity to the covenant. He has not kept the other Nazirite vows, but he has kept his hair uncut. Delilah cuts his hair, and he loses his strength. He is taken by his enemies and blinded. Later, he is brought out to be mocked by his enemies in the temple of Dagon, the local god. Samson prays for the strength to avenge himself, is granted that strength, and destroys the temple. He dies along with his enemies.

The writer does not tell the story of Samson simply to entertain. Discussing Samson's parents' negative reaction to his choice of a Philistine wife, the writer comments: "His father and mother did not know that this was from the LORD; for he was seeking a pretext to act against the Philistines. At that time the Philistines had dominion over Israel" (Judges 14:4).

While Samson was following his own tragic path to destruction, he was also beginning the struggle of his people for freedom from the Philistine oppressors, a struggle to be completed by David.

CCC, 2259–62; 2302: Killing and anger

34

Naomi and Ruth
READ RUTH

Your people shall be my people,
and your God my God.
RUTH 1:16

The book of Ruth tells the story of Naomi, a Hebrew woman, and her daughter-in-law Ruth. Because of famine, Naomi and her family leave Bethlehem and settle in Moab, the country across the Jordan. There Naomi's husband dies, and their two sons marry Moabite wives.

Then Naomi's two sons die. Naomi is troubled, knowing that she cannot stay in Moab with no one to protect her. She decides to return to Bethlehem and tells her daughters-in-law to return to the protection of their own families. One daughter-in-law, Orpah, returns to her family. The other, Ruth, stays with Naomi and asks not to be separated from her. In one of the most beautiful declarations of love and commitment found in the Bible, Ruth says to Naomi:

Do not press me to leave you
    or to turn back from following you!
Where you go, I will go;
    Where you lodge, I will lodge;
your people shall be my people,
    and your God my God.
Where you die, I will die—
    there will I be buried.
May the LORD do thus and so to me,
    and more as well,
if even death parts me from you!
      (Ruth 1:16–17)

Naomi relents and returns with Ruth to Bethlehem. There, in the midst of memories, Naomi becomes bitter and blames God for her misfortune. Ruth remains faithful to Naomi and goes into the fields to glean among the barley. (After the grain was harvested, the poor were permitted to go into the fields to gather any grain that was left behind.) While Ruth is working in the fields, she meets Boaz, the landowner, who is attracted to her and hears her story. Moved in his heart, he tells his workers to make sure that Ruth has plenty of grain to gather.

Upon returning home, Ruth tells Naomi of meeting Boaz. Naomi is delighted, because Boaz is a relative. She sends Ruth to meet him after the day's work. Ruth finds him sleeping, so she lies down next to him; and when he wakes up, she tells him that he is her relative. Boaz is pleased and wants to marry Ruth, but another relative has a closer relationship to her. Boaz works to remove all the legal barriers that keep him from marrying

Ruth. Once he does so, Boaz and Ruth marry and have a son. He is Obed, father of Jesse and grandfather of David.

The story of Ruth is that of God's *hesed*, or steadfast love, in the midst of family tragedy. Because of Ruth's faithfulness to Naomi and Boaz's steadfast love toward Ruth, the line to David was ensured.

CCC, 489: Exalting the lowly; 1611: Marriage

35

Hannah's Song
READ 1 SAMUEL 1:1–2:11

He raises up the poor from the dust.

1 SAMUEL 2:8

The story of the birth of Samuel is recounted in 1 Samuel 1:1–2:11. As is fitting for the man who will be the last of the judges and the anointer of kings, Samuel's birth is filled with wonder.

Elkanah, Samuel's father, has two wives, Peninnah and Hannah. Peninnah has a number of children. Hannah, the more beloved wife, has none, and she has to suffer the sneers of Peninnah. While praying at the shrine at Shiloh, Hannah pours out her troubles to God, promising that if she has a son, she will dedicate him totally to God. Eli, the priest of the shrine, notices her silent and painful prayer and accuses her of being drunk. Hannah defends herself: she is not drunk but is praying in sorrow and anxiety, asking for a son. Eli blesses her and prays that God will answer her petition. Relieved, Hannah returns to her husband, and soon they conceive a son.

When the son, Samuel, is born, Hannah wants to give him to God as soon as he is weaned. Her husband agrees. Finally, when Samuel is weaned, Hannah brings him to the chapel at Shiloh and places him under the care of Eli. In 1 Samuel 2:1–10, we find Hannah's song of thanksgiving.

> My heart exults in the LORD;
>> my strength is exalted in my God.
> My mouth derides my enemies,
>> because I rejoice in my victory.

> There is no Holy One like the LORD,
>> no one besides you;
>> there is no Rock like our God.
> Talk no more so very proudly,
>> let not arrogance come from your mouth;
> for the LORD is a God of knowledge,
>> and by him actions are weighed.
> The bows of the mighty are broken,
>> but the feeble gird on strength.
> Those who were full have hired themselves out
>>> for bread,
>> but those who were hungry are fat
>>> with spoil.
> The barren has borne seven,
>> but she who has many children is forlorn.
> The LORD kills and brings to life;
>> he brings down to Sheol and raises up.
> The LORD makes poor and makes rich;
>> he brings low, he also exalts.
> He raises up the poor from the dust;
>> he lifts the needy from the ash heap,

>   to make them sit with princes
>   and inherit a seat of honor.
>   For the pillars of the earth are the LORD's,
>   and on them he has set the world.
>   (1 Samuel 2:1–8)

If the song sounds familiar, it is because we also find its themes in the song of Mary, in Luke 1:46–55, as she celebrates her joy in being the mother of the Messiah.

CCC, 64: Holy women; 2578: Learning to pray

About: Women in Old Testament Times

The world of the Old Testament was patriarchal, but women were recognized as equal in the ways of God. In the second chapter of Genesis, written about 900 BC, the woman is seen as a necessary complement to the man, as a helpmate and companion (see Genesis 2:18). This image of the equality of man and woman is reflected in Genesis 1—written after Genesis 2—as both men and women are necessary to mirror the image of God (Genesis 1:27). In the Old Testament writers' understanding of existing relationships between men and women, the woman submitted to the man as a result of human sin (Genesis 3), a condition that later led to the practice of polygamy (Genesis 4:19).

At no time in the Old Testament could a woman be considered a man's equal. However, before the period of the Exile, women had a respected place in society. They served as prophets (Exodus 15:20; 2 Kings 22:14–20), judges (Judges 4–5), and queens. They were honored as models of wisdom (2 Samuel 14; 2 Samuel 20:16–22) and as mothers (Exodus 20:12; Deuteronomy 5:16). The Law protected the family rights of wives and mothers (Genesis 16:5–6).

Although marriages were arranged, there were instances of love and choice (Genesis 24:57–58; 24:67; 29:20). Women were not seen as property to be bartered. Incidents in which women are abused are found in stories describing the degraded state of the people when they were ignoring God.

In times after the Exile, when the written Law became more influential in the life of the people, the status of women declined. Circumcision was emphasized as a sign of the covenant, and women were seen as related to the covenant community thorough the male. The blood of the sacrifice became a means of atonement, and blood outside the ritual became unclean. While women who were menstruating were considered unclean and were excluded from worship, this later meant exclusion from society itself. The woman's place in worship was increasingly distant from the temple, and she could worship only through her husband.

A woman's vow was no longer considered as important as the vow of a male, and the husband could annul the vow of his wife (Numbers 30:1–2, 6–15). Women could not testify in court or speak to strangers, and they had to be veiled outside the home. They could not teach or be taught the Torah, and they were not to be educated. This was the state of women when Jesus began to teach, which highlights his extraordinary compassion toward them.

CCC, 64: Holy women; 489: Exalting the lowly

36

God Calls to Samuel

READ 1 SAMUEL 3

Samuel said, "Speak, for your servant is listening."
1 SAMUEL 3:10

Hannah gave her son, Samuel, to Eli for service in the chapel at Shiloh. She returns each year with an ephod, a linen garment that signifies Samuel's service. She continues to receive Eli's blessing and to bear children, having three more sons and two daughters.

While under Eli's care, Samuel grows in stature and esteem both in God's eyes and in the eyes of the people, but Eli's own sons neglect their duties and exploit the people. They prove themselves unworthy to follow Eli in the priesthood. Informed of their acts of blasphemy, Eli criticizes his sons, but they ignore him. (Samuel will have the same problem with his own sons; see 1 Samuel 8:1–5.)

In 1 Samuel 2:27–36, an unknown prophet comes to Eli and warns him that the days of his sons' abuses will soon come to an end. He tells Eli to raise up a faithful priest to take over his duties, as his family will be wiped out.

One night, when Samuel is sleeping, he hears a voice.

Then the Lord called, "Samuel! Samuel!" and he said, "Here I am!" and ran to Eli, and said, "Here I am, for you called me." But he said, "I did not call; lie down again." So he went and lay down. The Lord called again, "Samuel!" Samuel got up and went to Eli, and said, "Here I am, for you called me." But he said, "I did not call, my son; lie down again." Now Samuel did not yet know the Lord, and the word of the Lord had not yet been revealed to him. The Lord called Samuel again, a third time. And he got up and went to Eli, and said, "Here I am, for you called me." Then Eli perceived that the Lord was calling the boy. Therefore Eli said to Samuel, "Go, lie down; and if he calls you, you shall say, 'Speak, Lord, for your servant is listening.'" So Samuel went and lay down in his place.

Now the Lord came and stood there, calling as before, "Samuel! Samuel!" And Samuel said, "Speak, for your servant is listening." (1 Samuel 3:4–10)

What God tells Samuel is not a happy message. God is getting ready to act against Eli and his sons, and the time for their destruction is near. To his credit, Eli insists on hearing the truth and accepts God's will. Soon the Philistines attack, capture the Ark of the Covenant, and kill the sons of Eli. Upon hearing the news, Eli himself falls over and dies.

CCC, 2578: Learning to pray

37

Samuel and Saul

READ 1 SAMUEL 10–12

The LORD has anointed you ruler over his people Israel.
1 SAMUEL 10:1

Saul is a member of the tribe of Benjamin, the smallest of the tribes. He is described as handsome and tall, a man of substance. His father, a wealthy man, loses a number of donkeys. Saul goes in search of them but cannot find them. Told of a holy man in a nearby town, Saul goes to see him to ask if he can help Saul find the donkeys. Samuel is in the shrine of the town, conducting the sacrifices. When Samuel sees Saul, he realizes that Saul is the man God has told him about in a dream. God told Samuel that Saul is the man who will help free the people from the Philistines.

When Samuel tells Saul of God's plans for him, Saul does not believe him, as he is from a small tribe. Samuel confirms that Saul is God's choice and anoints him ruler of the people. Later Saul is proclaimed king in front of the assembled tribes.

Saul wins his first battles. When he defeats the Ammonites, his kingship is confirmed. Later, with the help of his son Jonathan, he defeats the Philistines. In the battle against the

Philistines, the Israelites were under pressure, and it looked as if they would run. They were discouraged because Samuel had not arrived to offer sacrifice. Saul offered the sacrifice himself to boost the morale of his men. When Samuel arrived, he was angry with Saul and told him that he had ruined his chances of being the permanent king of Israel.

In a later war, against the Amalekites, Saul again disobeys Samuel. In the judgment of war, Samuel ordered Saul in God's name to destroy the Amalekites: "Do not spare them, but kill both man and woman, child and infant, ox and sheep, camel and donkey" (1 Samuel 15:3). Saul defeats the Amalekites but does not follow Samuel's command. He captures the Amalekite king and spares his life. Saul also takes the best of the sheep, cattle, and lambs for himself and only destroys those he does not want. Saul thinks his own wants and needs are more important than the will of God, as given through his spokesman Samuel.

Samuel is furious with Saul. He hears the Lord say, "I regret that I made Saul king, for he has turned back from following me, and has not carried out my commands" (1 Samuel 15:11). When Saul brings the animals to sacrifice, Samuel asks, "Has the LORD as great delight in burnt offerings and sacrifices, as in obeying the voice of the LORD? Surely, to obey is better than sacrifice, and to heed than the fat of rams" (1 Samuel 15:22).

Although Saul repents, at least on the surface, he has failed God.

38

The Young David
READ 1 SAMUEL 16–17

*The spirit of the LORD came mightily upon
David from that day forward.*
1 SAMUEL 16:13

Samuel begins the search for a new king of Israel. God leads him to Bethlehem. There he meets Jesse to discover which of his sons God has chosen to replace Saul.

Jesse welcomes Samuel and, at his request, parades his sons before Samuel so he can see which one is God's choice. Seven of Jesse's sons meet Samuel, but God tells him that none of them will be king. Samuel asks Jesse if all his sons are present. He discovers that David is in the fields tending the sheep. Samuel has Jesse send for him. "He sent and brought him in. Now he [David] was ruddy, and had beautiful eyes, and was handsome. The LORD said, 'Rise and anoint him; for this is the one.' Then Samuel took the horn of oil, and anointed him in the presence of his brothers; and the spirit of the LORD came mightily upon David from that day forward" (1 Samuel 16:12–13).

There are two stories of how David came into Saul's service. In the first story, Saul is paying the price for his disobedience to God with terrific headaches and depression. He hears that David is a fine musician and singer and sends for him. Jesse sends David to Saul with a donkey loaded with gifts. David's singing and harp playing relieve Saul's headaches and depression (1 Samuel 16:23), and Saul makes David his armor bearer.

In the second and more famous story, Saul's armies are encamped across from a Philistine army. The Philistine champion Goliath comes and stands before the Israelite army every day and issues a challenge to anyone who will fight him in single combat.

The Israelite soldiers quiver with fear at the sight of him.

Meanwhile, Jesse sends David with supplies for his brothers in Saul's army and gifts for their commander. David is upset when he sees that no one will fight Goliath. He comes to Saul's attention. Saul questions David, who proclaims his willingness to face Goliath.

David faces Goliath without armor, which would hamper his movements. Selecting five smooth stones from a stream for his sling, David moves into battle.

Rushing the battle line, David puts a stone in his sling, whirls the sling over his head, and sends the stone into the middle of Goliath's forehead. Goliath falls forward and dies. David quickly takes Goliath's sword and cuts off his head. The amazed and demoralized Philistines run before the advancing Israelites. David proves to be the hero of Saul's armies.

39

David and Jonathan
READ 1 SAMUEL 18

The soul of Jonathan was bound to the soul of David, and
Jonathan loved him as his own soul.
1 SAMUEL 18:1

We all value friendship. A faithful friend can be a sure anchor and protector in the midst of chaotic or threatening situations. David had such a friend in Jonathan, Saul's most gifted son.

We first meet Jonathan in 1 Samuel 13. He commands one of Saul's regiments and is largely responsible for the defeat of the Philistines at Geba. Later, Jonathan slips into a Philistine camp and creates so much confusion that Saul orders a general attack, and ultimately the Israelites defeat them.

During the attack on the Philistines, Saul proclaimed an unwise oath, ordering his troops under pain of death not to eat anything until the Philistines were defeated. Jonathan did not hear the oath and ate some honey so he could fight on. Hearing afterward of his father's oath, Jonathan criticizes Saul, because his foolish oath allowed the Philistines to escape from the Israelites. Saul wants to kill Jonathan, but the army will not allow it.

After David kills Goliath, he becomes a trusted soldier of Saul, and he and Jonathan immediately become close friends. Jonathan makes a covenant with David, "because he loved him as his own soul" (1 Samuel 18:3). David will need this pledge of friendship.

Saul begins to hate David because he is successful. When David returns from battle, the women sing, "Saul has killed his thousands, and David his ten thousands" (1 Samuel 18:7). Saul tries to kill David but fails. Jonathan warns David to hide and pleads with Saul for David's life. Saul says that David will be spared, but he does not intend to keep that promise. Jonathan and Michal (Saul's daughter who is engaged to David) help David escape.

Jonathan later pledges his life to David. In return, he asks that David ensure the safety of his family. Jonathan recognizes, as Saul does not, that David will be the next king. Jonathan's friendship with David is more important to Jonathan than his own political ambition.

Later, both Saul and Jonathan die in battle. When David hears of Jonathan's death, he is filled with grief and sings:

> How the mighty have fallen
> in the midst of the battle!
>
> Jonathan lies slain upon your high places.
> I am distressed for you, my brother
> Jonathan;

greatly beloved were you to me;
   your love to me was wonderful,
   passing the love of women.

How the mighty have fallen,
   and the weapons of war perished!
      (2 Samuel 1:25–27)

40

Saul and David
READ 1 SAMUEL 24; 28

He [Saul] said to David, "You are more righteous than I; for you have repaid me good, whereas I have repaid you evil."
1 SAMUEL 24:17

Nothing can eat away at our lives worse than envy, especially the envy we feel when others succeed and we do not. We can also suffer the envy of others toward us when we accomplish something or have the good fortune to succeed where they have apparently failed. Envy was at the heart of Saul's bitter hatred of David, and his envy-fueled desire to destroy David led Saul to neglect his kingdom.

Running from Saul, David gathers a band of men and returns to Judea. He is too clever for Saul to catch. Saul destroys all who help David, including the family of the priest Ahimelech. The only surviving son, Abiathar, flees to David's protection.

In the campaign that follows, David twice has Saul at his mercy. The first time, David catches Saul in a cave in a vulnerable position. Instead of killing him, David cuts off a piece of his garment. The second time, David slips into Saul's camp and finds him asleep. This time David takes Saul's spear and water jug (1 Samuel 26:6–12). In each case, David explains that he will not kill Saul because Saul is the Lord's anointed. This also shows how politically shrewd David was. If David would not kill the Lord's anointed, he could expect the same protection and respect from others when he became king.

David attempts a final reconciliation with Saul, placing himself in jeopardy while doing so. The two men speak words of reconciliation, but after their meeting, David returns to the hills, no longer trusting Saul to keep his word.

As David grows stronger, Saul increasingly neglects his duties as king and turns against God. Before his final battle against the Philistines, Saul goes to an illegal fortune-teller to consult the dead. The message he gets from her is that he and his sons will die (1 Samuel 28:3–25).

After the battle, Saul, wounded by Philistine arrows, kills himself in despair. Killed with him are the faithful Jonathan and two of Saul's other sons. Finding Saul dead, the Philistines hang him up on a wall to shame him. But his body and those of his sons are rescued by Israelite soldiers and given a decent burial.

CCC, 1852: Sin

41

David and Abigail
READ 1 SAMUEL 25

David said to Abigail, "Blessed be the LORD,
the God of Israel, who sent you to meet me today!"
1 SAMUEL 25:32

In the time when he is being hunted by Saul, David and his followers survive by providing protection to farmers and sheepherders. One of the rich farmers he protects is Nabal. In return for protecting Nabal and his herds, David expects to be invited to the festival Nabal gives at the time of shearing the sheep. But Nabal refuses to invite David. In response, an angry David plans to visit Nabal with four hundred of his men and not leave anything alive.

Abigail, Nabal's wife, hears of Nabal's refusal and David's anger. To forestall David's attack, she gathers gifts of food and then goes to plead with him.

Abigail bows before David, reminding him that Nabal's name means "fool." Abigail calls David "prince" (1 Samuel 25:30) and tells him that the violence he has committed to this point will not reflect badly upon him because he has been fighting for the Lord. Since he has fought for the Lord, people will not seek revenge for the blood he has shed. However, if he kills Nabal over a personal insult, he will dishonor his reputation for justice.

David accepts Abigail's arguments and spares Nabal's life. When she returns to the estate, Abigail discovers that Nabal is drunk. She waits until morning to tell him: "In the morning, when the wine had gone out of Nabal, his wife told him these things, and his heart died within him; he became like a stone. About ten days later the LORD struck Nabal, and he died" (1 Samuel 25:37–38).

Nabal could have had a heart attack or a stroke; the text is not clear. After Nabal's death, David, admiring the wisdom and courage of Abigail, marries her.

Through Abigail, David learned an important lesson about the meaning of justice. He was being hunted down by the jealous Saul, yet he himself was about to kill Nabal out of spite. David recognized that through Abigail he received the message to restrain from violence. Abigail contributed to David's understanding of how to be a king in Israel. David was responsible to God for his actions and had to deal with the people justly and compassionately.

CCC, 1889: Charity; 2259–62: Killing;
2306: Renouncing violence

42

David the King

READ 2 SAMUEL 5–6

David danced before the LORD with all his might.

2 SAMUEL 6:14

David learns of the deaths of Saul and his friend Jonathan from an Amalekite who lies and says that he killed Saul (see 1 Samuel 31). The Amalekite is seeking to be rewarded, but instead David orders him to be killed. David needed to distance himself from any blame in their deaths. As the Lord's anointed, David wanted to emphasize the sacredness of the king who was appointed by God. In this way, he protected himself from those who might want to assassinate him.

David immediately moves to consolidate his authority. He goes to Hebron, where the tribe of Judah anoints him king. David then notifies the northern tribes of his anointing and calls on them to recognize him also. Saul was from the northern tribes, so they are inclined to be faithful to Saul's family.

Saul's general Abner establishes Saul's son Ishbaal as king of Israel. When it becomes obvious that David will win the civil war, Abner abandons Ishbaal, negotiates with David, and arranges for him to take Michal, Saul's daughter, as his wife. Thus, the northern tribes will be bound to David. Against David's orders, Joab, David's general, assassinates Abner, removing a potential rival. Ishbaal's own soldiers then kill him. David becomes the king of all the tribes of Israel.

David then moves to take Jerusalem. The city is under the control of the Jebusites, who insult David, believing that they are safe behind Jerusalem's walls. David captures the city with ease and makes Jerusalem his capital. Jerusalem, the "city of peace," becomes the center of political and spiritual life. David's choice of Jerusalem was politically astute, as Jerusalem had previously been under foreign control. David could say he had not favored any tribe in his choice for his capital.

David sends for the Ark of the Covenant and dances in joy when it is brought into the city. David's joy is spoiled by an argument with Michal, who criticizes him for dancing before the Ark. David sends her away, unwilling to have a son by a daughter of Saul who might eventually grow up to challenge him for the throne.

David is now at the height of his power. God promises in an everlasting covenant that David's house will continue. Overjoyed by this promise, David moves from success to success. However, as he succeeds, he begins to take personal credit for his good fortune and to forget the Lord.

Finally, David brings Jonathan's last living son, the lame Mephibosheth, to Jerusalem. Mephibosheth receives land for income and David's protection. David says that he is doing this to keep his promise to Jonathan. By keeping Mephibosheth close, David also reminds the northern tribes to be on their best behavior.

CCC, 2578–80: The prayer of the king

About: Jerusalem

Jerusalem means "city of peace," but because of its central significance in the religious life of Judaism, Christianity, and Islam, it has been a city that has had little peace. All three religions revere Jerusalem for its historical and symbolic importance. It is important for Judaism because it was the capital of David and Solomon and the home of the temple. The Western Wall in Jerusalem, where prayer is said daily, is the last surviving wall of Herod's temple. Christianity reveres Jerusalem as the place where Jesus was crucified and rose from the dead and where the early church experienced the coming of the Holy Spirit on Pentecost.

Islam also reveres Jerusalem. Muhammad instructed his early followers to pray facing Jerusalem before he later taught them to face Mecca. Jerusalem is the home of the Dome of the Rock, the shrine that marks the place from which Muhammad is believed to have taken his journey to heaven. All faithful Muslims hope to follow Muhammad on that journey.

In Old Testament times, Jerusalem was controlled by the Jebusites, enemies of the early Israelites. David conquered it around 1000 BC to serve as his capital. He made Jerusalem the worship center by bringing in the Ark of the Covenant, which held the tablets of the Law and was the center of devotion for all the tribes.

After David's death, Solomon built the temple in Jerusalem, in about 960 BC. He also linked the temple to his palace, doubling the size of the city. In the centuries that followed, Jerusalem was the fortress in which the people sought protection from the invading Assyrian armies. With the conquest and destruction of Jerusalem by the Babylonians, the people entered into exile lamenting what they had lost.

When the exiles returned to Jerusalem, they built a small temple and, under the direction of Nehemiah, a wall around the city. In the following centuries, the city was under siege many times until it was finally captured by the Romans in 63 BC. In 37 BC, the Romans appointed Herod the Great king of Judea, and he began construction of the great temple where Jesus prayed. Herod's city and temple were destroyed by the Romans in the Jewish-Roman War in AD 70.

Today Jerusalem has over seven hundred thousand inhabitants. It is a city of long memories and remains a place where Jews, Christians, and Muslims live in tension, praying for peace.

43

David, Bathsheba, and Nathan
READ 2 SAMUEL 11–12

David said to Nathan, "I have sinned against the LORD."
2 SAMUEL 12:13

It is easy for us to take credit when we succeed at something. We act as if the gifts we have received in life are ours by right. As David experiences more successes, he begins to act this way and to rule for himself instead of for God.

One day David goes out on the roof of the palace and sees Bathsheba bathing in the privacy of her home. He sends for her and sleeps with her, and she becomes pregnant.

Bathsheba's husband is Uriah, a Hittite in David's army who is fighting for him on the front lines. David sends for Uriah under the pretext of asking him how the battle is going. After Uriah gives his report, David sends him home to sleep with his wife, only to discover the next day that Uriah slept on the doorstep of the palace instead. Uriah did not think it was right for him to enjoy his home and his wife while his fellow soldiers were sleeping on the ground. David's plan to cover up his adultery has failed.

When Uriah returns to the front lines, David arranges for him to be killed in battle. Bathsheba laments Uriah's loss and after a period of mourning is taken in by David.

God is displeased, as is Nathan the prophet. Nathan goes to David with the following story:

> There were two men in a certain city, the one rich and the other poor. The rich man had very many flocks and herds; but the poor man had nothing but one little ewe lamb, which he had bought. He brought it up, and it grew up with him and with his children; it used to eat of his meager fare, and drink from his cup, and lie in his bosom, and it was like a daughter to him. Now there came a traveler to the rich man, and he was loath to take one of his own flock or herd to prepare for the wayfarer who had come to him, but he took the poor man's lamb, and prepared that for the guest who had come to him. (2 Samuel 12:1–4)

Enraged by the story of blatant injustice, David pronounces a sentence against the man. Then Nathan accuses David of being the man who abused the gifts of God by taking Bathsheba.

To his credit, David admits his sin (see Psalm 51), and he is forgiven. However, his first child by Bathsheba dies, and Nathan foretells that David's selfishness will bring trouble into his home. "Thus says the LORD: I will raise up trouble against you from within your own house; and I will take your wives before your eyes, and give them to your neighbor, and he shall lie with your wives in the sight of this very sun" (2 Samuel 12:11).

CCC, 1422–26: Penance and reconciliation

44

David and Absalom

READ 2 SAMUEL 18

O my son Absalom, my son, my son Absalom!
Would I had died instead of you.
2 SAMUEL 18:33

David's children cause him pain and grief. Like Eli and Samuel before him, David raises children who are not worthy of him. David loves his children to distraction and unfortunately does not discipline them. His oldest son and heir, Amnon, violates David's trust by tricking David into sending Amnon's half sister, Tamar, to see him alone. Amnon rapes Tamar and sends her away. David is angry with Amnon, but he does not punish him.

Absalom, Tamar's full brother, takes Tamar into his home and plots the murder of Amnon. Finally, he invites Amnon to a feast and has him killed. Absalom flees into exile. There Absalom remains, until Joab intervenes and David calls Absalom back to court, but not into his presence.

When David gives Absalom permission to return to Jerusalem, he does not know (or does not care) that he is giving Absalom an opportunity to promote himself at David's expense. Absalom goes into the city and sets himself up as a judge. When ruling on a case, Absalom makes sure that those who come from the North win especially favorable judgments. In this way, he divides the kingdom between North and South and plans to lead the northern tribes in rebellion.

With the help of some of David's officers, Absalom attacks David. David escapes, but Absalom takes control of Jerusalem. He soon controls David's women as well, as Nathan prophesied.

Although Absalom seems to have won, David is the greater warrior and general. Absalom's armies fall into a trap set by David and are destroyed. As Absalom tries to escape, he is caught in the branches of a tree by his long hair. Against David's wishes, Joab drives a spear through the helpless Absalom's heart. David is victorious but realizes that he is paying the price for his sins. He has no victory celebration but weeps for the son he has loved and lost.

CCC, 1858: Sin; 2197–2200: Parents and children

45

David's Later Years

READ 2 SAMUEL 19–24

The LORD lives! Blessed be my rock.

2 SAMUEL 22:47

David's troubles do not end with Absalom's death. Most of Absalom's supporters are from the northern tribes in Israel. Defeated with Absalom, they realize that they have to return to David but are hesitant. As the two southern tribes in Judah show their support of David, the ten northern tribes complain bitterly.

> "Why have our kindred the people of Judah stolen you away, and brought the king and his household over the Jordan, and all David's men with him?" All the people of Judah answered the people of Israel, "Because the king is near of kin to us. Why then are you angry over this matter? Have we eaten at all at the king's expense? Or has he given us any gift?" But the people of Israel answered the people of Judah, "We have ten shares in the

king, and in David also we have more than
you. Why then did you despise us? Were we
not the first to speak of bringing back our
king?" But the words of the people of Judah
were fiercer than the words of the people of
Israel. (2 Samuel 19:41–43)

The bitter differences between North and South smolder
under the strong central authority of David—and, later,
Solomon— and will eventually divide the kingdom.

David's last years are troubling. He fights against the
remnants of the rebellious tribes of the North. God sends a
plague on Israel because David conducts a census to know
the strength of his kingdom, a knowledge that belongs to
God alone.

David was a great poet and a person of deep, yet flawed,
spirituality. He is credited with a heartfelt song of faith in
God for his continued protection (2 Samuel 22). In this song,
David describes God as a rock, fortress, deliverer, shield, horn,
stronghold, and refuge. God's actions in David's life are like
the mighty forces of nature aiding him: breakers surge and
floods overwhelm; the earth sways and shakes, trembles and
quakes. David's enemies flee and are destroyed, ground into the
dust and trampled. God's commitment to David will not end,
though David is unfaithful in many ways. God's covenant love
is steadfast and enduring.

CCC, 2578–80: The prayer of the king

46

The Wisdom of Solomon
READ 1 KINGS 3

*Give your servant therefore an understanding
mind to govern your people.*
1 KINGS 3:9

David dies after a forty-year reign and is succeeded by
Solomon, his son by Bathsheba. Solomon begins his rule
by making alliances with his neighbors. He first makes sure
that there will be peace with Egypt by marrying a daughter of
Pharaoh. Other alliances bring some one thousand wives and
concubines into Solomon's house. Unfortunately, Solomon also
builds shrines to the wives' personal gods that will distract the
Israelites from worship of the true God.

When praying at Gibeon, Solomon experiences God's
presence and asks him for wisdom to rule the people well:
"And your servant is in the midst of the people whom you have
chosen, a great people, so numerous they cannot be numbered
or counted. Give your servant therefore an understanding mind
to govern your people, able to discern between good and evil;
for who can govern this your great people?" (1 Kings 3:8–9).

God is pleased with this request and promises to give Solomon a wise and discerning mind so that he can rule the people with justice and fairness. God also promises Solomon a long life with riches if Solomon will continue to walk in God's ways and follow the teachings of the Law.

Solomon's gift of wisdom is soon put to the test. Two women come to him for judgment. They live in the same house and gave birth to infants within three days of each other. One woman's child died in the night. She then took her dead child and placed it on the other woman's breast, taking the live child in return. When the woman whose child had not died awoke, she saw that she had been given the dead child of the other mother.

> Now both women stand before the king claiming to be the mother of the living child, with only their word as proof of the truth. "So the king said, 'Bring me a sword,' and they brought a sword before the king. The king said, 'Divide the living boy in two; then give half to the one, and half to the other.' But the woman whose son was alive said to the king—because compassion for her son burned within her—'Please, my lord, give her the living boy; certainly do not kill him!' The other said, 'It shall be neither mine nor yours; divide it.' Then the king responded: 'Give the first woman the living boy; do not kill him. She is his mother.'" (1 Kings 3:24–27)

Hearing of this incident, all of Israel praises God for giving them a king who is able to make the right decisions.

CCC, 1676: Pastoral wisdom

About: The Temple

M ost of us have a special place where we go to think, to dream, and to plan. We do not usually share this place with others, especially if it is a place where we pray. This place is sacred to us. The temple was such a place for the Jewish people. There they would meet God and celebrate God's presence in their midst.

The temple was where the people offered sacrifices so that God could be praised and worshiped. When the people sinned or defiled the temple, driving out God's presence, offerings of atonement had to be made.

The temple was especially important for celebrating the three principal feasts: the Passover, or the Feast of Unleavened Bread; the Feast of Weeks, celebrated at the beginning of the wheat harvest; and the Feast of Booths, celebrated when the harvest and produce were gathered.

Solomon built the first temple. This was not the first shrine to God; local shrines had been built in Mamre, Shechem, Gibeah, Gilgal, and Shiloh. Solomon built the temple to fulfill the promise of David and to centralize the worship of the people in Jerusalem. In his reforms, Josiah (c. 640–609 BC) emphasized this purpose of the temple. Solomon's temple stood, with renovations and repairs, until its destruction by the Babylonians in 587 BC.

When the exiles returned from Babylon, they built a second temple that was completed abut 515 BC. Modeled on Solomon's temple, it was not nearly as magnificent, but it fulfilled the same purpose as the earlier temple. Since the Jewish people no longer had a king, the role of high priest became especially important. In the period of the second temple, the high priest and his staff virtually governed the internal affairs of the people. Hence, the appointment of the high priest became a political as well as a religious issue.

Herod the Great (37 BC–AD 4) leveled the second temple to build a new and more magnificent structure. The central shrine of the temple remained much the same, but Herod added an enormous platform within a broad public area. A Roman colonnade surrounded this vast complex of buildings, and the people entered through enormous gates. This was the temple where Jesus prayed.

Herod wanted to win the allegiance of the people with his temple and to show the importance of his kingdom. The temple did not last far beyond his reign. It was destroyed by the Romans in the year 70.

CCC, 1081: Worship of God;
1093–94: The old covenant prefigures the new

47

Solomon Builds the Temple
READ 1 KINGS 8

Even heaven and the highest heaven cannot contain you,
much less this house that I have built!
1 KINGS 8:27

Solomon divides the kingdom into twelve administrative districts. He conscripts workers from eleven of these districts to work one month a year to supply the needs of the court. The text suggests that Judah was spared the burden of supplying conscripted labor. This preferential treatment of Judah makes the northern tribes resentful. To make matters worse, Solomon erases some tribal boundary lines. This redistricting will eventually lead the northern tribes to rebel.

In order to get the materials he needs to build the temple, Solomon makes a treaty with King Hiram of Tyre, who has access to the cedars of Lebanon and the stone quarry. Solomon provides the king with agricultural products in return for the materials and the labor to cut the trees. In addition to hiring the Lebanese laborers, Solomon conscripts thirty thousand Israelites from the northern part of the kingdom to work on the temple.

The temple takes seven years to build. Most of the stonework is done in the quarry so that nothing will disrupt the sacredness of the temple. The carved stones are transported from the quarry and assembled in Jerusalem. The stone is of the finest quality. The splendor of the temple is revealed in the detailed descriptions of the wood (olive, fir, imported cedar) used to decorate the interior, which is also filled with gold.

The temple has three main rooms. Beginning with the entry hall, it continues to the sanctuary, where the altar of incense and the table of bread are located. Finally, there is the Holy of Holies, the most interior part of the temple, where the Ark of the Covenant, containing the tablets of the Ten Commandments, is kept. Also in the Holy of Holies are two gold-plated wooden cherubim whose extended wings reach from wall to wall.

When the temple is finished, representatives from the whole nation gather to celebrate the dedication. Sheep and oxen are sacrificed, and the Ark of the Covenant is brought in procession to its resting place in the Holy of Holies. "And when the priests came out of the holy place, a cloud filled the house of the LORD, so that the priests could not stand to minister because of the cloud; for the glory of the LORD filled the house of the LORD" (1 Kings 8:10–11).

The sign of God's presence and Solomon's prayer of dedication seal the temple as the central place of worship for the kingdom. They also support Solomon's throne as the keeper of God's sacred space. After a final round of sacrifice and seven days of festivities, the people return home, satisfied with the temple and with their king.

CCC, 583–86: Jesus and the temple

About: Sacrifice in the
Old Testament

When the temple was the center of religious life, the principal form of worship was sacrifice. This included offering clean animals (cattle, sheep, goats, doves, pigeons) for slaughter, roasting, and eating, and offering grains, bread, or incense. In sacrifices involving animals, they were killed and dismembered. At least part of the animal (usually the fat) was burned on the altar, and the priest either sprinkled or smeared the blood on the altar.

People offered sacrifice for a number of reasons. When a person who had sinned wanted to restore the relationship with God, a complete animal was sacrificed as a burnt offering, or holocaust. The man offering the sacrifice laid his hands on the victim's head, signifying his complete submission to God. In this way, atonement was accomplished.

Other types of animal sacrifice were done to reestablish peace or well-being between God and the person offering the sacrifice. In this case, the dismembered animal was divided between God, the priest, and the person. The fat was burned as an offering to God. The priest and the offering person divided the rest of the meat. This established a communion between God and the person. It could be a thanksgiving offering, a fulfillment of a vow or promise made to God, or a free-will offering.

There were also sin offerings and guilt offerings. In sin offerings, the blood of the animal was placed on the horns of the altar of sacrifice, symbolizing the removal of sin and impurity from the altar, giving the person or the whole people access to God once again. The rest of the blood was poured out at the base of the altar, symbolizing the return or restoration of the life of the animal to its creator.

In cases where a person or a community realized that it did not deliberately offend God but that the relationship with God was disordered, guilt offerings were made. These offerings of atonement might be made if, for example, a person came into contact with the unclean. (Note that *clean* and *unclean* as they are used in the Old Testament are ritual terms for what is suitable or unsuitable. The terms do not refer to physical cleanliness.)

The intent of sacrifice was for the people to recognize their total commitment to God, that God shared life with the people, and that the people were sinful and needed atonement. When the interior meaning of sacrifice was ignored, the prophets criticized the practice. After the destruction of Herod's temple, the Jewish people made sacrifice an act of daily offering their prayers and deeds to God.

CCC, 613–14: The sacrifice of Christ

48

Solomon Neglects God
READ 1 KINGS 11

For when Solomon was old, his wives
turned away his heart after other gods.
1 KINGS 11:4

Solomon's kingdom flourishes. In an episode celebrated in the Old Testament, the queen of Sheba comes to view the wealth of the kingdom, giving Solomon many gifts and receiving many gifts in return. The queen praises Solomon for his wealth, and she considers him lucky to live in such favor with God.

1 Kings 10 continues with descriptions of Solomon's wealth and how he liked to spend money on himself and his close followers. He especially loved gold. "All King Solomon's drinking vessels were of gold, and all the vessels of the House of the Forest of Lebanon were of pure gold; none were of silver—it was not considered as anything in the days of Solomon. For the king had a fleet of ships of Tarshish at sea with the fleet of Hiram. Once every three years the fleet of ships of Tarshish used to come bringing gold, silver, ivory, apes, and peacocks" (1 Kings 10:21–22).

The rest of the chapter celebrates the material riches that flowed into the kingdom. "The whole earth sought the presence of Solomon to hear his wisdom, which God had put into his mind. Every one of them brought a present, objects of silver and gold, garments, weaponry, spices, horses, and mules, so much year by year" (1 Kings 10:24–25).

It seemed a glorious time to be a member of God's people. The riches of Solomon were thought to be signs of God's favor. Yet these were examples of the rot that was seeping into the kingdom. 1 Kings 11 tells the story of how Solomon began to move away from his faith in God. With the one thousand wives he married comes their beliefs, and their closeness to Solomon leads to their influence on his faith. "For when Solomon was old, his wives turned away his heart after other gods; and his heart was not true to the LORD his God, as was the heart of his father David. . . . Then Solomon built a high place for Chemosh the abomination of Moab, and for Molech the abomination of the Ammonites, on the mountain east of Jerusalem. He did the same for all his foreign wives, who offered incense and sacrificed to their gods" (1 Kings 11:4, 7–8).

Solomon's abandonment of his faith in God leads to trouble. God promises Solomon that while he lives, David's kingdom will not be destroyed. But upon his death, the kingdom will be divided, leaving his descendants with only the kingdom of Judah.

CCC, 2087–89: Protecting our faith

49

The Division of David's Kingdom

READ 1 KINGS 12:1–19

The king answered the people harshly. He disregarded the advice that the older men had given him.

1 KINGS 12:13

In the last years of his rule, Solomon forgets the promises he made to God. Foreign wives and their gods dominate his house. Solomon himself sacrifices to foreign gods within the walls of his castle. He also alienates the ten tribes in the north by using them for forced labor. When he was building the temple, this was perhaps forgivable. However, Solomon also built a palace for himself and his wives and concubines that was much larger. Even more irritating to the northern tribes is that the people of Solomon's own tribe of Judah are not conscripted to work.

After Solomon's death, his son Rehoboam inherits the throne. When representatives from the ten northern tribes complain about the unfair labor practices, Rehoboam goes to the elders in Judah for advice. The elders tell Rehoboam to go easy on them and to change the labor practices. If Rehoboam serves the tribes instead of dictating to them, they will be his servants forever.

The advice of Rehoboam's younger counselors is more insulting. They advise that Rehoboam demand even more of the workers. When Rehoboam meets with the representatives of the northern tribes, he follows the advice of the younger counselors, telling the representatives of the northern tribes: "My father made your yoke heavy, but I will add to your yoke; my father disciplined you with whips, but I will discipline you with scorpions" (1 Kings 12:14).

The northern tribes of Israel have had enough. Rehoboam's taskmaster is stoned to death. Rehoboam barely escapes with his life, and the northern tribes send for Jeroboam to be the king of the new kingdom of Israel.

Rehoboam pays for his arrogance by ruling over a small and weakened Judah. He continues to battle with the northern tribes, now the kingdom of Israel, whose border is only 109 miles from Jerusalem. His stubbornness will drain his resources.

While Rehoboam is distracted with his fight with Israel, the Egyptians take advantage of his weakness and raid Judah. They conquer Jerusalem, sack the temple, and force Rehoboam to pay a huge ransom before they will withdraw. Rehoboam buys off the Egyptians, but the war with Israel will last forty years.

50

Jeroboam Is King of Israel

READ 1 KINGS 11:26–40; 12:20–13:34

So the king took counsel, and made two calves of gold.

1 KINGS 12:28

Jeroboam was a member of the northern tribe of Ephraim. Because he was a man of obvious talent and ability, Solomon chose him to be the taskmaster of the forced laborers. Jeroboam diligently carried out his duties until he met the prophet Ahijah on the road outside Jerusalem, and Ahijah foretold the end of Solomon's kingdom. Ahijah saw ten northern tribes establishing the new kingdom of Israel. He also prophesied that Jeroboam would become king of Israel and would remain so as long as he worshiped God alone. When Solomon heard of this, he sought to kill Jeroboam, who had to go into hiding in Egypt until Solomon died.

After Solomon's death, Jeroboam returns to the northern region and is anointed king of Israel. After fortifying the border cities of Shechem and Penuel, Jeroboam seeks to take away the religious and political influence of Judah by setting up two rival temples, in Dan and Bethel. In these he places two golden bulls, introduces a new priesthood not limited to the priestly tribe of the Levites, and establishes a new worship calendar. He also promotes worship in other "high places" in Israel. Jeroboam no doubt sees the golden bulls as symbols of the presence of the invisible God, but later generations will worship the bulls themselves as idols. Because of this, Jeroboam's memory will be condemned.

A prophet from the southern kingdom of Judah criticizes Jeroboam's actions. In a dramatic showdown, Jeroboam challenges the Judean prophet and stretches out his hand to condemn him. Instead, Jeroboam's hand shrivels up. Acknowledging that the prophet is in touch with the power of God, Jeroboam asks to have his hand restored, and it is. Yet in spite of this warning, Jeroboam is obstinate and does not change his policies.

Jeroboam's stubbornness leads to the condemnation of his temple and his house. When near death, Jeroboam sends his wife in disguise to consult with Ahijah, the old prophet who originally proclaimed his rule of Israel. Ahijah promised Jeroboam long life if he followed God. However, his actions have doomed him and all the males of his house. As a sign of this, Jeroboam's infant son, Abijah, immediately dies. Jeroboam dies after a reign of twenty-two years.

The history of the kings of the northern kingdom of Israel will be one of dynastic changes and bloody coups. The biblical writers will see this as the natural consequence of Jeroboam's decision not to be faithful to God.

About: Ahab, Jezebel, and the Gods of Canaan

When Jeroboam died, his son Nadab took over rule of Israel. In less than two years, Baasha murdered Nadab, along with the rest of Jeroboam's sons. Baasha ruled for about twenty-four years and was succeeded by his son Elah. Elah was murdered by Zimri, who committed suicide in seven days. His successor was his general Omri, whose family would rule through four kings.

Under Omri and his son Ahab, Israel was prosperous and internationally respected. Omri built a new capital at Samaria. Ahab built an enormous fortress to protect his houses and belongings. He married Jezebel, the daughter of the king of Tyre. She is called a Sidonian in the text. Jezebel was an enthusiastic supporter of the storm god, Baal, and his consort, the goddess Asherah. While worship of these gods was probably popular in Israel before Jezebel, Ahab made it official. He erected an altar for Baal and shrines for Asherah. "Ahab did more to provoke the anger of the LORD, the God of Israel, than had all the kings of Israel who were before him" (1 Kings 16:33).

Baal was a particularly important god in the eyes of his followers because he was associated with the storms that brought the yearly rainfall to the semiarid Canaan. Baal was the god of the yearly cycle of fertility and plant growth. He was depicted as restoring divine order over drought. In his epic battle with Mot, the god of death, Baal was victorious and won the title "rider of the clouds."

The prophet Elijah was an enemy of the worship of Baal. Elijah saw that the fertility rites of Baal, which probably included sacred prostitution, corrupted faith in God. In the worship of Baal, the powers of nature were seen as divine. Elijah taught that God was a universal being who was not a "nature god" trapped in the unchanging seasonal cycles. For Elijah, it was important to show that God, not Baal, was the one who controlled the storms and brought the seasonal rains.

This is the background to the intense struggle between Elijah and God on the one side and Ahab and Jezebel and the Canaanite gods on the other, a struggle that will continue throughout the time of the prophets of the period before the Exile.

CCC, 279–80; 282–89: God the creator

51

Elijah Is Fed by God

READ 1 KINGS 17

*She went and did as Elijah said, so that she as well as he and
her household ate for many days.*

1 KINGS 17:15

Elijah ("Yahweh is my God") was a prophet in the northern
kingdom of Israel. He is quickly introduced and predicts in
God's name that a drought will come over Israel. The drought is
to last for three years, creating an agricultural crisis and leading
the people to question the power of the Canaanite gods.

After this proclamation, Elijah is sent by God to live in a
wadi. (A wadi is a deep gully or streambed that is dry except
during the winter rains.) God promises that Elijah will be fed
there and will drink from the streams. "So he went and did
according to the word of the LORD; he went and lived by the
Wadi Cherith, which is east of the Jordan. The ravens brought
him bread and meat in the morning, and bread and meat in
the evening; and he drank from the wadi. But after a while
the wadi dried up, because there was no rain in the land"
(1 Kings 17:5–7).

Elijah is then sent to a widow in Zarephath, in the kingdom of Sidon, the heartland of the cult of Baal. When he finds the woman, Elijah asks her for water and a morsel of bread. The widow replies that she barely has enough for herself and her son; she is going home to prepare a last meal. Elijah promises that if she will use what she has to feed him, God will provide for her. Elijah, the woman, and her family eat for many days from the jar of meal and the jug of oil in the woman's house.

After a period of time, the widow's son dies. Elijah picks up the boy and prays. "He cried out to the LORD, 'O LORD my God, have you brought calamity even upon the widow with whom I am staying, by killing her son?' Then he stretched himself upon the child three times, and cried out to the LORD, 'O LORD my God, let this child's life come into him again.' The LORD listened to the voice of Elijah; the life of the child came into him again, and he revived. Elijah took the child, brought him down from the upper chamber into the house, and gave him to his mother; then Elijah said, 'See, your son is alive'" (1 Kings 17:20–23).

These stories show the way God was preparing Elijah for his task. In the midst of drought, Elijah was fed. In the heartland of the cult of Baal, God also provided food for those who believed in his word and that of his prophet.

CCC, 2581–84: Elijah and conversion

About: Prophets and Prophecy

Early prophets, who would forecast the future for a fee, were common in the Near East. People would go to a shrine where a prophet lived to seek knowledge about the future. The prophet, or oracle, would usually fall into a trance and then tell the petitioner what he foresaw when he came back to reality. Saul sought one of these prophets when he was searching for his father's donkeys (1 Samuel 9:9–13). Kings also had professional prophets to help them make policy decisions.

The classic prophets of the Old Testament were different. They did not so much predict the future as proclaim God's covenant love. They did not foretell specific events but made clear the consequences the people would face if they did not repent and reform their lives.

The classic prophets cared deeply about the people. The suffering of the poor especially angered them, as they saw God's vision for the people being ignored by those in power who failed to follow the obligations of covenant love. The prophets were activists attacking those who abused God's moral law.

The prophets of Israel and Judah were also intercessors, bringing God's word to the people and bringing the concerns of the people to God. They pleaded with God to give the people one more chance, to delay the punishment that was sure to come. However, the word of God needed to be proclaimed. It demanded decisive action, repentance, and commitment.

Many of the prophets have books written in their name. They are sometimes listed as major or minor prophets in the

Bible. These labels have to do with the length of the books and do not indicate the prophet's importance.

Prophets came from all walks of life. Amos was a shepherd and a tree trimmer. Hosea lamented his unfaithful wife. First Isaiah was a court aristocrat. Micah was a small-town man uncomfortable in the city. Jeremiah was a reluctant man drafted by God. Ezekiel came from a family of priests. The prophets also performed symbolic, dramatic acts. Isaiah walked in the clothes of a slave to get his message across. Jeremiah wore a yoke like an ox would wear to proclaim his message that Judah must submit to the power of Babylon.

All of the classic prophets were called to represent God by bringing his concerns to the attention of the people and communicating what would be in store for them if they chose to ignore God's word.

CCC, 61–64: God forms his people Israel

52

Elijah Confronts Baal
READ 1 KINGS 18

Then the fire of the LORD fell and consumed the burnt offering.
1 KINGS 18:38

God now calls Elijah to confront Ahab and pagan gods. He is going into enemy territory: Jezebel is killing off the prophets of Israel. In spite of the danger, Elijah is not put off. When he meets with the king, Ahab calls Elijah the "troubler of Israel." Elijah responds by challenging the priests of Baal and Asherah to a contest with the God of Israel.

The 450 priests of Baal and 400 priests of Asherah sponsored by Jezebel gather with Elijah on Mount Carmel. Elijah orders that two bulls be brought up. One bull is taken by the pagan priests and laid upon the sacrificial altar, surrounded by wood. The other bull is taken by Elijah to be prepared for sacrifice. Elijah then tells the priests of Baal and Asherah to pray to their gods to light the wood of sacrifice.

The priests of Baal pray in frenzy to their god. Elijah mocks them, saying Baal must be asleep. This drives the priests to even greater fury. "Then they cried aloud and, as was their custom, they cut themselves with swords and lances until the blood gushed out over them. As midday passed, they raved on until the time of the offering of the oblation, but there was no voice, no answer, and no response" (1 Kings 18:28–29).

Elijah then prepares his sacrifice. He builds an altar with twelve stones, signifying the twelve tribes of Israel. Then the prophets of Israel dig a trench around the altar, put in the wood, and pour water over the altar three times so that it soaks the wood and fills the trench. Elijah then prays to God to answer him so that the followers of Baal will know he speaks for God and will turn their hearts back to God. "Then the fire of the Lord fell and consumed the burnt offering, the wood, the stones, and the dust, and even licked up the water that was in the trench. When all the people saw it, they fell on their faces and said, 'The Lord indeed is God; the Lord indeed is God'" (1 Kings 18:38–39).

Elijah orders that the priests of Baal be killed. Then the rains begin. Elijah, believing that Ahab has been converted back to faith in the true God, triumphantly leads him home.

CCC, 2581–84: Elijah and conversion

53

The Still Small Voice

READ 1 KINGS 19

Go out and stand on the mountain before the LORD, for the
LORD is about to pass by.

1 KINGS 19:11

Elijah's feeling of triumph after the contest with the prophets
of Baal and Asherah is short-lived. He discovers that the
real holder of political power in Israel is Queen Jezebel. Upon
hearing that the priests of Baal and Asherah have been defeated
and killed on Mount Carmel, Jezebel sends a message to Elijah
saying that by the next day he will be dead.

Elijah flees in terror. He goes south to Beersheba, beyond
Jezebel's influence. Then he dismisses his servant and goes into
the wilderness. Depressed, he asks God to let him die. "It is
enough; now, O LORD, take away my life, for I am no better
than my ancestors" (1 Kings 19:4).

But God is not ready to take Elijah and provides food for
him. Elijah goes further into the wilderness of Mount Horeb
(Sinai) for forty days of fasting and prayer. While Elijah is
praying in a cave, God comes to him once again and asks him
what he is doing there. Elijah desperately replies that he feels

he is the only one left in Israel who is willing to speak for God, and God's enemies are seeking his death. In reply, God calls Elijah out of the cave to meet with him.

> He said, "Go out and stand on the mountain before the LORD, for the LORD is about to pass by." Now there was a great wind, so strong that it was splitting mountains and breaking rocks in pieces before the LORD, but the LORD was not in the wind; and after the wind an earthquake, but the LORD was not in the earthquake; and after the earthquake a fire, but the LORD was not in the fire; and after the fire a sound of sheer silence. When Elijah heard it, he wrapped his face in his mantle and went out and stood at the entrance of the cave. Then there came a voice to him that said, "What are you doing here, Elijah?" (1 Kings 19:11–13)

God tells Elijah that with a few more acts, his ministry to God will be at an end.

Elijah's encounter with God shows how God was beginning to go beyond the wild displays of power such as mighty thunder, lightning, and storms. God revealed himself to be more than a storm God who might be compared with any other god. The word of God would now and in the future be found in the communication of the divine word to his prophets.

CCC, 2581–84: Elijah and conversion

54

Elisha and the Healing of Naaman

READ 2 KINGS 2; 5

His flesh was restored like the flesh of a young boy,
and he was clean.

2 KINGS 5:14

Elijah finds his successor, Elisha, after his experience of God on Mount Horeb. Elisha is following behind a plow pulled by twelve yoke of oxen, a sign that he is a prosperous farmer. Elijah calls Elisha to become a prophet by throwing his cloak over Elisha's head. Elisha immediately agrees, slaughters the oxen, boils them, and gives them to the people to eat. As it becomes apparent that Elijah is going to leave, Elisha stays close by him, not wanting to lose his mentor. Just before Elijah is taken up into heaven, Elisha asks for a double portion of Elijah's spiritual gifts, and they are given to him.

Elijah's departure from the earth is vividly described in 2 Kings 2:11–12. While Elijah and Elisha are walking by the Jordan, a chariot of fire separates them, and Elijah ascends into heaven. After Elijah disappears, Elisha takes up Elijah's cloak to continue his ministry.

Elisha works to complete Elijah's mission of bringing down the house of Ahab. Elisha supports a new leader, Jehu, who defeats Ahab, killing him, Jezebel, and as many members of their family as he can find. Elisha also performs many miracles, perhaps the most familiar involving Naaman, the commander of the army of the king of Aram. Naaman suffers from leprosy. When he hears of a miracle-working prophet in Israel, he goes to visit him in hopes of a cure.

When Naaman arrives at Elisha's house, Elisha does not even see him, but simply tells him through a messenger to wash on the banks of the Jordan River. Naaman is upset. Are there not enough rivers in his homeland to wash in? Disgusted, he prepares to leave, but his servants plead with him, saying: "Father, if the prophet had commanded you to do something difficult, would you not have done it? How much more, when all he said to you was, 'Wash, and be clean'?" (2 Kings 5:13).

Naaman sees the sense of their argument, goes into the Jordan River, and is cleansed of his leprosy. This healing leads Naaman to believe in God. Elisha does not accept payment for his part in the healing, declaring that it was all done for the Lord.

This story and the other miracle stories about Elisha show God's power as demonstrated by his prophet to be a central element in the life of Israel. When the people refused to follow the guidance of true prophets, they would lose themselves and their nation. The northern kingdom of Israel was soon conquered by the Assyrian Empire.

About: Assyria

It is no fun to live in a neighborhood dominated by a bully or by gangs. It spoils the day to know that at any moment you could be put upon and pressured into doing something you do not want to do. The kingdoms of Israel and Judah knew that feeling, as the Egyptians, the Assyrians, and the Babylonians pushed them around.

The Assyrian Empire was centered in the land that is in present-day northern Iraq. The Assyrian Empire lasted from about 1900 BC to about 612 BC. There were periods in which they were not aggressive against their neighbors. In other periods, as we see in the Bible, they expanded their conquests and their influence over their neighbors. They supported themselves through agriculture, trade, and, between 930 BC and 612 BC, conquest. The Assyrians were proud of their brutality, as the following inscription of an Assyrian emperor shows: "Like the Thunderer [the storm god Adad] I crushed the corpses of their warriors in the battle that caused their overthrow. I made their blood to flow over all the ravines and high places of mountains. I cut off their heads and piled them up at the walls of their cities like heaps of grain. I carried off their booty, their goods, and their property beyond reckoning."

Under ambitious rulers like Ashurnasirpal II (883–859 BC) and Shalmaneser III (859–824 BC), Assyria expanded into Canaan to control the trade routes to Egypt. Israel formed alliances with Aram and the Phoenician cities to stop them but was defeated in battle. The Israelite kings bought peace by paying tribute. Assyria was content to sit back and take the money.

Under the rule of Tiglath-pileser III (745–727 BC), Assyria expanded further, quickly gaining control over Babylon. Israel and Syria once again tried to unite to shake off the Assyrians. They stopped paying tribute and put armies in the field. Tiglath-pileser III's successor, Shalmaneser V (726–722 BC), invaded Canaan again, destroying Syria and capturing Samaria, the capital of Israel, in 722 BC. Sargon II (722–705 BC) completed the destruction of the northern kingdom of Israel by retaking Samaria and deporting most of the inhabitants.

During the reign of Sennacherib (705–681 BC), Assyria invaded Judah, capturing most of the kingdom and besieging Jerusalem.

Later, weakened by external pressure and by internal conflict, the Assyrian Empire fell to the forces of Babylon, Media, and Scythia. The capital city of Nineveh fell in 612 BC. The remnants of the Assyrian armies were defeated in 605 BC in the battle of Carchemish.

55

Amos Denounces Empty Religion

READ AMOS 5

Hear this word that I take up over you in lamentation,
O house of Israel.

AMOS 5:1

The northern kingdom of Israel prospers after the overthrow of Ahab. During the reign of Jeroboam II (786–746 BC), Israel is rich and powerful. By all human measures, the kingdom is a success. The country is expanding, trade with surrounding countries is active, and religion is popular. However, belief in God continues to be joined with the fertility cult of the false god Baal. The people think that their growing richer is a sign of God's blessing.

The wealthy and powerful landowners use their influence to build large estates at the expense of family farms. They go to court to cancel the claims of the families who have owned the farms for generations. Then they build larger plantations and turn the farmers into their slaves. These same landowners think to please God by offering sacrifices. The practice of religion is increasing, but with no sense of what it means to be morally responsible.

Amos is a herdsman from Judah who works in Israel tending sycamore fig trees, the small fruit of which is eaten by the poor. He becomes angry at the oppression of the poor and criticizes the court prophets who promote religion but forget morality, who pander to the worst instincts of their employers instead of calling for repentance. Amos speaks against the rich and morally insensitive, telling them what God thinks of those who would offer sacrifice yet oppress the poor.

Amos promises the rulers of Israel that they will lose their land and be surrounded by enemies, stripped of their defenses, and plundered (Amos 3:11). Their rich wives will also suffer. Amos calls them "cows of Bashan" who in their leisure consume the fruits of other people's labor, offering nothing in return. They will be led out hooked to one another to serve new masters (Amos 4:1–2).

Amos sums up God's message in an oracle in 5:21–24. An oracle is a message of God spoken through a prophet. Speaking through Amos, God tells the people:

> I hate, I despise your festivals,
> > and I take no delight in your solemn
> > > assemblies.
> Even though you offer me your burnt
> > offerings and grain offerings,
> > I will not accept them;
> and the offerings of well-being of your fatted
> > animals
> > I will not look upon.

> Take away from me the noise of your songs;
>> I will not listen to the melody of your
>>> harps.
> But let justice roll down like waters,
>> and righteousness like an ever-flowing
>>> stream. (Amos 5:21–24)

God's words to the people tell of harsh judgment. Amos also holds out hope for the future, when a pruned, repentant people will return to the Lord (Amos 9:11 15).

> I will restore the fortunes of my people
>> Israel,
>>> and they shall rebuild the ruined cities
>>>> and inhabit them;
>> they shall plant vineyards and drink their
>>> wine,
>>>> and they shall make gardens and eat
>>>>> their fruit.
> I will plant them upon their land,
>> and they shall never again be plucked up
>>> out of the land that I have given them,
>>>> says the Lord your God.
>>>>> (Amos 9:14–15)

CCC, 1807: Justice; 1829: Charity; 1889: Love of neighbor

56

Hosea and His Unfaithful Wife

READ HOSEA 1–2

The LORD said to Hosea, "Go, take for yourself a wife of whoredom and have children of whoredom."

HOSEA 1:2

The northern kingdom of Israel turned from God and fell to the Assyrians in 722 BC. The prophet Hosea was called by God to experience the tragedy of Israel in his own life. Hosea had an unfaithful wife named Gomer. His struggle with their relationship was at the heart of his prophecy. God called Hosea to see in his personal struggle an example of how God was trying to deal with an unfaithful people.

Hosea and Gomer have three children. Hosea names their first son Jezreel, after the place where Ahab's family was killed by Jehu, an event that symbolized the eventual fall of Israel. The second child, a daughter, is named Loruhamah, which means "no mercy": God's mercy has been temporarily removed from the nation. The second son is named Loammi, "not my people," meaning that the people are not acting as though they are God's unique possession. These names show the growing distance of Israel from God, in favor of the false gods and rituals of Canaan.

When Gomer leaves Hosea, God sends him to bring her back. In the same way, God will bring back the people of Israel each time they stray. God looks upon Israel as if the nation is his bride. Hosea speaks of God's distress over the behavior of the people.

> Hear the word of the Lord, O people of
> Israel;
> for the Lord has an indictment against
> the inhabitants of the land.
> There is no faithfulness or loyalty,
> and no knowledge of God in the land.
> Swearing, lying, and murder,
> and stealing and adultery break out;
> bloodshed follows bloodshed.
> (Hosea 4:1–2)

The kings and priests think that they are pleasing God with their sacrifices, but Hosea makes it clear that it is justice and not sacrifice that pleases God: "For I desire steadfast love and not sacrifice, the knowledge of God rather than burnt offerings" (Hosea 6:6).

Hosea is the prophet of divine love that will not give up on the sinner. If only the people would repent, God would turn his anger from them. "I will heal their disloyalty; I will love them freely, for my anger has turned from them" (Hosea 14:4).

CCC, 2099–2100: True sacrifice

About: The Kingdom of Judah

After his escape from the northern kingdom, Rehoboam was accepted by the two southern tribes of Judah as their king. Rehoboam was enraged at his treatment by the northern tribes and was determined to get his revenge against the new kingdom of Israel. While he spent his resources fortifying his northern borders against Israel, he ignored the growing threat from Egypt. Egypt attacked Jerusalem. They invaded the palace, taking the treasure Solomon had spent so much time accumulating, and stripped the temple of its gold plating and shields (1 Kings 14:25–26). Rehoboam had to be satisfied with shields of bronze. The Egyptians made no effort to control Judah but seem to have been satisfied with what they stole.

Judah kept the war with Israel going for a number of generations. Israel was the greater and more powerful kingdom, so Judah had to strip itself of resources to keep pace. The memory of Rehoboam's bitterness made them fight against their northern relatives instead of forming a natural alliance with them.

Judah's kings were of the house of David. This meant that the social order in Judah was relatively stable. This stability was helped by the religious conviction that God had made a covenant with David, promising to support his throne and to establish descendants after him.

Jehoshaphat (873–849 BC) finally established peace between Israel and Judah, with Jehoshaphat's son Jehoram marrying Athaliah, daughter of Ahab. Israel's king Jehu killed Jehoram's son Ahaziah and his retinue of forty-two relatives.

Athaliah, Ahaziah's mother, claimed the crown and ruled for about six years. Joash, the last surviving member of Ahaziah's family, was kept in hiding. Joash was put forward as ruler by his supporters at seven years of age. Athaliah was taken out of power and killed in 837 BC.

Joash was murdered by his servants, and his son Amaziah was in turn murdered by the sons of those servants. Uzziah (Azariah) took over from Amaziah, his father, and reigned for fifty-two years. In his last seven years he stayed in seclusion because of leprosy, and his son Jotham ruled as regent. After Jotham's reign, Ahaz became king, and instead of supporting Israel and Syria against the Assyrians, he paid tribute to Assyria, making Judah a vassal state. This move was severely criticized by Isaiah because it brought Assyrian gods into the temple. However, it probably preserved Judah from the destruction suffered by Syria and Israel.

Ahaz was not faithful to God, engaging in such contemptible practices as sacrificing one of his sons in the Canaanite way (2 Kings 16:1–4). When Ahaz died, he was replaced by his surviving son, Hezekiah. Hezekiah tried to make up for his father's unfaithfulness.

Hezekiah at first continued to pay tribute to Assyria. Then he turned against Assyria, openly rebelling in 705 BC. Leading a coalition of small neighboring nations against Assyria, Hezekiah was at first successful but was finally overwhelmed by Assyria's superior forces. Sennacherib, the Assyrian king, invaded Judah and swept away all before him. As for Hezekiah, Sennacherib "made him a prisoner in Jerusalem, his royal residence, like a bird in a cage."

Jerusalem withstood the siege in 701 BC, not the least because Hezekiah had the foresight to secure the water supply of the city before he set out on his military adventures. When counseled to surrender the city, Hezekiah instead listened to the prophet Isaiah, who declared that the Lord would defend the city (2 Kings 19:34). While the city itself was not destroyed, much of Judah was transferred to cities loyal to Assyria, and Hezekiah had to pay a huge sum to buy off the Assyrians. "Hezekiah gave him all the silver that was found in the house of the LORD and in the treasuries of the king's house" (2 Kings 18:15).

57

Isaiah's Vision
Read Isaiah 6

Woe is me! I am lost, for I am a man of unclean lips.
ISAIAH 6:5

Being a prophet carries a personal cost. Isaiah (c. 760–701 BC), probably the best-known and most beloved prophet in the Old Testament, gives a vivid description of what it means to experience the presence of God and the humility it takes to speak for God.

The year is 742 BC. Uzziah (Azariah) has died, and the nation of Judah feels a sense of loss. In a vision, Isaiah sees God as a king surrounded by the heavenly court. Isaiah describes God as sitting on a throne surrounded by seraphs, heavenly guardians with three sets of wings. With one set of wings they cover their faces, overwhelmed by God's glory; the second set covers their nakedness out of respect for God. With the final set of wings, they carry God's messages to the world.

Awed to be in the presence of God, Isaiah cries: "Woe is me! I am lost, for I am a man of unclean lips, and I live among a people of unclean lips; yet my eyes have seen the King, the LORD of hosts!" (Isaiah 6:5).

In response, one of the seraphs flies to Isaiah with a live coal taken from the altar and touches his lips with it, declaring that his guilt has departed. Isaiah then hears the voice of the Lord saying, "Whom shall I send, and who will go for us?" And Isaiah replies, "Here am I; send me!" (Isaiah 6:8).

Isaiah's mission is to a people who listen but do not comprehend; who look but do not understand. They are a people who refuse to hear the voice of God. With their hearts hardened and their senses dulled, they will suffer the full measure of the consequences of their actions.

CCC, 208: The glory of God

About: The Three Isaiahs

There is only one book of Isaiah in the Bible, but it is actually three collections of sayings by three prophets. Each of the collections was written in a distinct time in history as each of the prophets faced the problems of his period.

The first collection, Isaiah 1–39, is the work of the great prophet himself, who prophesied in Judah from 742 to 701 BC. His disciples saved his messages and brought them into Babylon during the Exile. Included in Isaiah's collection were the sayings of other preexilic prophets.

In Babylon, when the people were living without a temple and a royal family, the priestly editors had time to rework the original messages of the prophets to meet their new religious situation. They added words that the original prophets had not said. They added sayings that the disciples of the prophets said at a later time.

A member of a community that reverenced the name of Isaiah wrote the second major collection, Isaiah 40–55. Second Isaiah wrote for the people in exile. His message is one of hope: the people have suffered enough; they have been forgiven and will move from sadness to joy. The first words of Second Isaiah (Isaiah 40:1) are remembered each year when the opening of Handel's oratorio *Messiah* is played around Christmas: "Comfort, O comfort my people."

The final collection, Isaiah 56–66, was written after the people were freed from exile in 539 BC. They had returned to desperately poor villages in Judah. The straight road they had been promised was filled with many ruts. They were in a more somber, penitential mood. The third prophet to write in the name of Isaiah called them to hope. The God who had rescued them would not leave them now.

58

Isaiah's Message
READ ISAIAH 1–2

*Your princes are rebels
and companions of thieves.*
ISAIAH 1:23

The people of Judah do not understand the moral implications of the covenant, so they oppress the poor. Isaiah believes that the root of their uncaring attitude is the practice of idol worship:

> Ah, sinful nation,
>   people laden with iniquity,
> offspring who do evil,
>   children who deal corruptly,
> who have forsaken the LORD,
>   who have despised the Holy One of
>   Israel,
>   who are utterly estranged! (Isaiah 1:4)

Even temple sacrifice is tainted because the people do not obey God's law:

> Trample my courts no more;
>> bringing offerings is futile;
>>> incense is an abomination to me.
>>>> (Isaiah 1:12–13)

Human pride is the downfall of the people:

> The haughty eyes of people shall be brought low,
>> and the pride of everyone shall be humbled;
> and the Lord alone will be exalted
>> in that day.
> For the Lord of hosts has a day
>> against all that is proud and lofty,
>> against all that is lifted up and high.
>>>> (Isaiah 2:11–12)

Isaiah reacts in horror over the oppression of the poor by the wealthy classes and the ruling princes of Judah:

> Your princes are rebels
>> and companions of thieves.
> Everyone loves a bribe
>> and runs after gifts.
> They do not defend the orphan,
>> and the widow's cause does not come
>>> before them.

> Therefore says the Sovereign, the Lord of
>> hosts, the Mighty One of Israel:

> Ah, I will pour out my wrath on my
> enemies,
> and avenge myself on my foes!
> I will turn my hand against you;
> I will smelt away your dross as with lye
> and remove all your alloy.
> And I will restore your judges as at the first,
> and your counselors as at the beginning.
> Afterward you shall be called the city of
> righteousness,
> the faithful city. (Isaiah 1:23–26)

He explains how the situation in the land is looked upon by God:

> For the vineyard of the LORD of hosts
> is the house of Israel,
> and the people of Judah
> are his pleasant planting;
> he expected justice,
> but saw bloodshed;
> righteousness,
> but heard a cry! (Isaiah 5:7)

Isaiah makes it clear that the people have plenty to think about. He is battling for the souls of the chosen people, whose hearts are hardened and who choose to ignore God.

CCC, 238; 544: God's love for the poor

59

A Savior Will Come
READ ISAIAH 9; 11

For a child has been born for us,
a son given to us.
ISAIAH 9:6

It is a sad experience to watch someone self-destruct. In our lives, we see marriages going bad, friends taking drugs, alcoholism destroying a family. We can be discouraged watching people make bad decisions and ignore all our efforts to help. Life goes on, but we feel helpless because we want to make a difference and are ignored.

This is how Isaiah must have felt in his nearly forty-year ministry as a prophet. In his life, he saw the destruction of Israel, the pagan practices of King Ahaz, the invasion of Judah by the Assyrians. Isaiah constantly warned the kings and religious authorities about the consequences of their actions, and they constantly ignored him.

Isaiah, however, continued to believe in God, and he believed that there would be a time when an anointed one (a messiah) would come to accomplish God's word in the world.

In the time of Judah's deepest distress, Isaiah says to Ahaz,

> For a child has been born for us,
>   a son given to us;
> authority rests upon his shoulders;
>   and he is named
> Wonderful Counselor, Mighty God,
>   Everlasting Father, Prince of Peace.
>   (Isaiah 9:6)

Hezekiah, the child born to Ahaz and his successor, is a disappointment to Isaiah. Therefore, Isaiah begins to speak of the characteristics of the hoped-for and future king, who will better serve God and bring about a full measure of divine blessing on the land:

> A shoot shall come out from the stump of
>   Jesse [David's father],
>   and a branch shall grow out of his roots.
> The spirit of the Lord shall rest on him,
>   the spirit of wisdom and understanding,
>   the spirit of counsel and might,
>   the spirit of knowledge and the fear of
>   the Lord.
> His delight shall be in the fear of the Lord.
>
> He shall not judge by what his eyes see,
>   or decide by what his ears hear;

but with righteousness he shall judge the
poor,
and decide with equity for the meek of
the earth. (Isaiah 11:1–4)

The familiar ring to these texts shows that Isaiah was prophesying deeper than he knew. In the Christmas liturgy, the church will use his teaching to capture the wonder of the birth of Jesus.

CCC, 497: Mary's virginity; 712: Awaiting the Messiah

60

Micah's Call for Justice
READ MICAH 6

What does the LORD require of you?
MICAH 6:8

M icah prophesied at the same time as First Isaiah. While Isaiah prophesied from the court of Jerusalem, Micah was probably an elder in a small village in Judah.

Micah can see the abuses the rich and politically connected are committing against the poor: "They covet fields, and seize them; houses, and take them away; they oppress householder and house, people and their inheritance" (Micah 2:2). And while the rulers are doing this, they listen to their court prophets and practice their temple sacrifices, believing that they are following the Lord. They criticize Micah for preaching God's judgment.

In response, Micah charges that the critics are mistaken about their relationship with God, since they do not care for the poor, especially women and children. Micah teaches that because of their behavior, they have brought judgment upon themselves.

Hear this, you rulers of the house of Jacob
    and chiefs of the house of Israel,
who abhor justice
    and pervert all equity,
who build Zion with blood
    and Jerusalem with wrong!
Its rulers give judgment for a bribe,
    its priests teach for a price,
    its prophets give oracles for money;
yet they lean upon the LORD and say,
    "Surely the LORD is with us!
    No harm shall come upon us."
Therefore because of you
    Zion shall be plowed as a field;
Jerusalem shall become a heap of ruins,
    and the mountain of the house a wooded
        height. (Micah 3:9–12)

What God really wants, Micah says, is for them to remember the covenant. God took them from slavery to freedom, and they are being called to treat one another with the same compassion that God has shown them.

"With what shall I come before the LORD,
    and bow myself before God on high?
Shall I come before him with burnt
        offerings,
    with calves a year old?

Will the Lord be pleased with thousands of
    rams,
    with ten thousands of rivers of oil?
Shall I give my firstborn for my
    transgression,
    the fruit of my body for the sin of my
    soul?"
He has told you, O mortal, what is good;
    and what does the Lord require of you
but to do justice, and to love kindness,
    and to walk humbly with your God?
    (Micah 6:6–8)

CCC, 2259: The consequences of sin

About: Care for the Poor

We hear many reasons why people are poor. In too many cases, the poor are unfairly blamed for their poverty. This is not the case in the Old Testament. The majority of its witnesses see poverty as an affliction brought about by human selfishness and greed.

The Old Testament taught people to give special protection and care to the poor. The wealthy were to give them loans without interest (Deuteronomy 23:19–20), periodically release them from their debts (Deuteronomy 15:1–6), release those bonded to them with provision for their welfare (Deuteronomy 15:12–18), and leave them part of the harvest (Deuteronomy 24:19–22).

In the history of Israel and Judah, these stipulations were more ignored and violated than followed. The kings especially were responsible for relieving the needs of the poor. They failed to do so and more often than not cooperated with the wealthy to oppress the poor. In the end, it was the wealthy who lost everything, being exiled to Babylon, and the poor who remained in the land.

The prophets were especially strong in criticizing the wealthy and proclaiming God's concern for the poor. They did not think that poverty was the result of chance. Rather, it was the result of the wealthy breaking the covenant. The rich used their wealth not for the good of all but for their own purposes. In doing this, they broke the covenant with God and called God's judgment upon themselves, as proclaimed by the prophets.

The psalms add a different dimension to the place of the poor, emphasizing the poor's total dependence on God because they had so little. They were the righteous in contrast with their oppressors, who were considered the "unrighteous ones."

However, the psalms do not celebrate poverty as a good in itself. It is clear that the poor prayed to God for deliverance. They expected to be found guiltless by God. They were not willing to submit, as if their oppressors had the right to treat them unjustly. But they knew they would only find deliverance in God's way and in God's time. Only in God could they find justice.

In Luke 4:16–21, Jesus summarizes these Old Testament themes to identify his own mission. He came to meet the needs of the poor as the fulfillment of his Father's will.

CCC, 64; 238; 489; 544; 559: God's concern for the poor

61

The Promised Ruler from Bethlehem

READ MICAH 5

O Bethlehem . . .
from you shall come forth for me
one who is to rule in Israel.

MICAH 5:2

We remember one prophecy from Micah because it appears in the Christmas story. The second chapter of Matthew tells the story of the wise men from the East searching for the promised Messiah. They go to the palace of Herod for help in finding the child. Herod is frightened and consults with the chief priests and scribes for the answer. They respond, "In Bethlehem of Judea; for so it has been written by the prophet: 'And you, Bethlehem, in the land of Judah, are by no means least among the rulers of Judah; for from you shall come a ruler who is to shepherd my people Israel'" (Matthew 2:5–6).

Micah wrote this verse as a song of hope. In Micah 5:1, he predicted the ultimate degradation of the king of Judah: "Now you are walled around with a wall; siege is laid against us; with a rod they strike the ruler of Israel upon the cheek."

In spite of this insult to the king and, through the king, to the whole people of Judah, Micah believes in the faithfulness of God. However, the salvation from David's house will not come from the center of political power but from the margins: "But you, O Bethlehem of Ephrathah, who are one of the little clans of Judah, from you shall come forth for me one who is to rule in Israel, whose origin is from of old, from ancient days" (Micah 5:2).

Bethlehem was the birthplace of David. Micah sees a new king fulfilling God's promises to David. God's help will come with the king born in David's line. "And he shall stand and feed his flock in the strength of the LORD, in the majesty of the name of the LORD his God. And they shall live secure, for now he shall be great to the ends of the earth; and he shall be the one of peace" (Micah 5:4–5).

Micah's prophecy was a word of hope intended to give comfort to the people in the midst of their troubles. In his vision, Micah saw God intervening in human affairs as the One who would bring peace and harmony. What Micah could not imagine was the depth and breadth of God's response to the people and to the whole human family.

About: Hope in the Old Testament

In the Old Testament, the people's hope was based on their confidence that God would provide. God would provide what they needed to live, the peaceful land flowing with milk and honey (Genesis 15:7; 17:8; Exodus 3:8, 17), and judges and kings to protect them from danger. After Israel and Judah fell, a new king was promised who would be a more complete protector than David.

The people hoped for justice, that the good would be rewarded and the wicked punished: "See, a king will reign in righteousness, and princes will rule with justice" (Isaiah 32:1).

Hope was based on God's assurance that he would not abandon the people; they would live in peace and harmony. "The wolf shall live with the lamb, the leopard shall lie down with the kid, the calf and the lion and the fatling together, and a little child shall lead them" (Isaiah 11:6).

The people lost hope when they placed their confidence in idols, treaties with foreign nations, and ritual ceremonies rather than adopting an internal attitude of obedience to God. "So be careful not to forget the covenant that the LORD your God made with you, and not to make for yourselves an idol in the form of anything that the LORD your God has forbidden you" (Deuteronomy 4:23).

The strongest words of hope came from the prophets when all seemed lost. Israel and Judah had been destroyed, but a remnant would be saved. "On that day I will raise up the booth of David that is fallen, and repair its breaches, and raise up its ruins, and rebuild it as in the days of old" (Amos 9:11).

Hope is the virtue that kicks in when nothing else seems to help. Reflecting on the continued hope of the people of Israel and Judah in the face of disaster helps us recognize that real hope is not about wishes and fantasies. It is about relying on God—the same God who brought the chosen people out of despair.

CCC, 1817–21: The virtue of hope

62

The Rule of Manasseh
READ 2 KINGS 21

I am bringing upon Jerusalem and Judah such evil that the ears
of everyone who hears of it will tingle.
2 KINGS 21:12

Judah survived the Assyrian invasion with Jerusalem intact, but the land and the people were impoverished. While Assyria dominated, Hezekiah died, and his son Manasseh became king. Manasseh (687–642 BC) would be king longer than any other Judean or Israelite king. He was in a difficult situation, trying to preserve some independence for Judah and knowing that the kingdom could be crushed at any moment.

Hezekiah made some attempts to reform the religion of Judah, and the people hope that Manasseh will follow his lead. Instead, Manasseh rebuilds the local pagan shrines and sponsors a program to combine elements of the worship of God with the worship of Baal. Even worse, Manasseh defiles the temple, building altars to Baal in its sacred precincts. Manasseh also builds a chapel in the name of Baal's consort, Asherah, where sacred prostitution is practiced.

Assyrian religious practices are also promoted, even in the temple. The worship of the sun, the moon, and the stars as deities is introduced, as is the cult of the dead, a practice long condemned. Manasseh sanctions astrology, magic, and divination. Finally, he resorts to the monstrous practice of human sacrifice, burning his son as an offering to win the pagan god's favor in a time of emergency (see Jeremiah 7:31).

Reflecting on the rule of Manasseh, a later editor of 2 Kings will see in Manasseh's actions the seeds of the ultimate downfall of Judah.

> The LORD said by his servants the prophets, "Because King Manasseh of Judah has committed these abominations, has done things more wicked than all that the Amorites did, who were before him, and has caused Judah also to sin with his idols; therefore thus says the LORD, the God of Israel, I am bringing upon Jerusalem and Judah such evil that the ears of everyone who hears of it will tingle. I will stretch over Jerusalem the measuring line for Samaria, and the plummet for the house of Ahab; I will wipe Jerusalem as one wipes a dish, wiping it and turning it upside down. I will cast off the remnant of my heritage, and give them into the hand of their enemies; they shall become a prey and a spoil to all their enemies, because they have done

what is evil in my sight and have provoked
me to anger, since the day their ancestors
came out of Egypt, even to this day." (2 Kings
21:10–15)

Manasseh deserted God, ushering in a dark age in Judah's
religious history. The people of Judah would have to pay the
price of his infidelity.

CCC, 1902–4: Legitimate authority

63

Nahum Celebrates the Fall of Nineveh

READ NAHUM

Nineveh is like a pool
whose waters run away.
NAHUM 2:8

Even when Assyria was powerful, it was a fragile empire based on fear and intimidation. Because of internal conflict and powerful enemies like the Medes and the Babylonians, the capital of Assyria, Nineveh, was sacked in 612 BC. The Assyrian Empire fell apart between 611 BC and 605 BC. The prophet Nahum ("comfort") lived in this time of Assyria's disintegration.

While others see political powers at work, Nahum sees the judgment of God in the impending destruction of Nineveh and shares his satisfaction in it:

> Nineveh is like a pool
>> whose waters run away.
> "Halt! Halt!"—
>> but no one turns back.

"Plunder the silver,
    plunder the gold!
There is no end of treasure!
    An abundance of every precious thing!"
        (Nahum 2:8–9)

There is no question in Nahum's mind that Nineveh and the Assyrians will receive just punishment for what they have done to Judah and Israel. God will pour out his wrath on them like a stream of fire, and Nineveh's walls will fall. While he expresses joy over the destruction of Nineveh, Nahum also sees God as a stronghold and a refuge for all who believe in him.

With Nineveh and the Assyrians destroyed, Nahum sees a bright future for Judah: "Look! On the mountains the feet of one who brings good tidings, who proclaims peace! Celebrate your festivals, O Judah, fulfill your vows, for never again shall the wicked invade you; they are utterly cut off" (Nahum 1:15).

In the short term, Nahum's hopes for Judah will not be fulfilled: Jerusalem will be sacked and the temple destroyed less than fifty years after his death.

When we read the fearsome images of God in Nahum, it is important to remember that the "wrath of God" as described in the Old Testament is a symbol that shows the distance between God's holiness and human sinfulness. For Nahum, the fall of Nineveh is a sign of what will happen to all who oppress the poor and a sign of God's passionate concern for justice. For those concerned with justice for the oppressed, God's call for justice is good news. For those not concerned with justice and compassion, it is a day of judgment.

CCC, 210: God's mercy

64

Zephaniah Attacks Complacency
READ ZEPHANIAH

I will punish the people . . .
who say in their hearts,
"The LORD will not do good,
nor will he do harm."
ZEPHANIAH 1:12

Pope John Paul II called Catholics to a new evangelization. He was especially concerned about Catholics who live in countries like ours with a high standard of living. Prosperity has led to complacency and religious indifference, with people not caring about the needs of the world or about their own relationship with God. Zephaniah ("Yahweh protects") was called to minister in a religious situation like this.

A contemporary of Nahum, Zephaniah did not feel as hopeful about Judah as Nahum did. Zephaniah sounds a warning to those who seem to be indifferent to the changes Manasseh made. Zephaniah tells the people that God is judging Judah for continuing the practice of worshiping pagan gods. This goes past the limits of God's tolerance.

While detailing God's anger against those who actively promote the worship of other gods, Zephaniah is especially critical of the religiously indifferent. They do not seem to care what is taught or believed, as long as they are left alone.

> At that time I will search Jerusalem with
> lamps,
> and I will punish the people
> who rest complacently on their dregs,
> those who say in their hearts,
> "The LORD will not do good,
> nor will he do harm."
> Their wealth shall be plundered,
> and their houses laid waste.
> Though they build houses,
> they shall not inhabit them;
> though they plant vineyards,
> they shall not drink wine from them.
> (Zephaniah 1:12–13)

For all who disobey the Lord, either actively or through indifference, Zephaniah foresees a fearsome day of judgment.

> That day will be a day of wrath,
> a day of distress and anguish,
> a day of ruin and devastation,
> a day of darkness and gloom,

a day of clouds and thick darkness,
 a day of trumpet blast and battle cry
against the fortified cities
 and against the lofty battlements.
 (Zephaniah 1:15–16)

But after making these judgments over all creation, Zephaniah ends with a song of hope.

The LORD, your God, is in your midst,
 a warrior who gives victory;
he will rejoice over you with gladness,
 he will renew you in his love;
he will exult over you with loud singing
 as on a day of festival.
I will remove disaster from you,
 so that you will not bear reproach for it.
I will deal with all your oppressors
 at that time.
And I will save the lame
 and gather the outcast,
and I will change their shame into praise
 and renown in all the earth.
At that time I will bring you home,
 at the time when I gather you;
for I will make you renowned and praised
 among all the peoples of the earth,
when I restore your fortunes
 before your eyes, says the LORD.
 (Zephaniah 3:17–20)

Zephaniah's voice needs to be heard to shake people out of their complacency. He is a prophet whose words speak to us today as we are called to a new evangelization.

CCC, 2094: Offenses against God's love

65

King Josiah's Reform
READ 2 KINGS 23

The king . . . made a covenant before the LORD,
to follow the LORD, *keeping his commandments, his decrees,
and his statutes, with all his heart and all his soul.*

2 KINGS 23:3

King Manasseh of Judah dishonored his faith and his nation. Judah was corrupt, pagan gods received royal protection, and human sacrifice was practiced. There was an obvious need for reform. When Manasseh died in 642 BC, his son Amon continued his father's practices but ruled for only two years before being assassinated. His son Josiah, who was only eight years old, succeeded Amon. Josiah would grow up to become one of Judah's great kings. "He did what was right in the sight of the LORD, and walked in all the way of his father David; he did not turn aside to the right or to the left" (2 Kings 22:2).

At the age of twenty, Josiah rules in his own name. With the power of Assyria dwindling, Judah is ready to act independently without fear of invasion. Josiah begins a major religious reform.

He first orders the renovation of the temple. He puts the entire temple tax into the hands of the workers to use in repairing the temple. "But no accounting shall be asked from them for the money that is delivered into their hand, for they deal honestly" (2 Kings 22:7).

Seeing that Josiah is sincere in his desire to reform, the high priest Hilkiah reports that an ancient text of the Law has been found in the temple and sends it to be read to Josiah. When Josiah hears the reading of the Law, he tears his clothes in distress. He determines to implement the reforms that the Law calls for.

The book that was read to Josiah was probably an early edition of the book of Deuteronomy. Following the book as a guide, Josiah has all shrines to pagan gods destroyed; ends the cults to the stars, the sun, and the moon; and ends cult prostitution. He then reinstates the celebration of the Passover in Jerusalem.

Politically, Josiah uses the weakness of Assyria to regain much of the territory that was controlled by David and Solomon. The people in the lands of the former kingdom of Israel are forced to acknowledge that true worship can take place only in the temple in Jerusalem. In this way, Josiah combines worship with his royal authority.

Josiah is killed in 609 BC when he contests the passage of Egyptian armies through Canaan to assist the Assyrians in their final battle. His body is brought back to Jerusalem, and he is buried in his own tomb.

CCC, 2437–41: The right ordering of society

About: The Rise of Babylon

These words of the prophet Habakkuk reflect the Jewish experience of the Babylonians:

> Look at the nations, and see!
> > Be astonished! Be astounded!
> For a work is being done in your days
> > that you would not believe if you were told.
> For I am rousing the Chaldeans,
> > that fierce and impetuous nation,
> who march through the breadth of the earth
> > to seize dwellings not their own.
> Dread and fearsome are they;
> > their justice and dignity proceed from
> > > themselves.
> Their horses are swifter than leopards,
> > more menacing than wolves at dusk;
> > their horses charge.
> Their horsemen come from far away;
> > they fly like an eagle swift to devour.
> They all come for violence,
> > with faces pressing forward;
> > they gather captives like sand.
> At kings they scoff,
> > and of rulers they make sport.
> They laugh at every fortress,
> > and heap up earth to take it.
> Then they sweep by like the wind;

> they transgress and become guilty;
> their own might is their god!
> (Habakkuk 1:5–11)

The city of Babylon was located on the left bank of the Euphrates River, not far from the present-day city of Baghdad, in Iraq. Babylon was the center of a vast empire that at its height controlled the territory covering present-day Iraq, Syria, and Israel. Babylon's economic base was agricultural. It continued the efforts of previous civilizations to control the floods of the great Tigris and Euphrates rivers by creating canals and reservoirs to irrigate its fields.

The Babylonians were ruled by a series of kings known as the Chaldeans (625–538 BC), who allied themselves with the Medes to defeat the Assyrians and to destroy the Assyrian capital of Nineveh.

With Assyria gone, there was a political vacuum. At first, this helped the kingdom of Judah, as King Josiah was able to expand Judah's control over most of Canaan. However, Judah's independence was short-lived. Having defeated the Egyptians who had come to the aid of the diminishing Assyrians at Carchemish (605 BC), King Nebuchadnezzar cleared the way for Babylonia to become the dominant power in the Fertile Crescent. Babylon quickly made Judah a client kingdom. Judah now had to pay tribute to a new master.

To follow up his victory against the Egyptians at Carchemish, Nebuchadnezzar overreached himself by invading Egypt. In the ensuing battle with the Egyptians, the Babylonians retreated. Judah dreamed of liberation. Judah's decision to rebel against Babylonian rule would lead to its own destruction.

66

Habakkuk's Reprimand

READ HABAKKUK

There is still a vision for the appointed time. . . .
If it seems to tarry, wait for it.

HABAKKUK 2:3

The defeat of the Assyrians and the emergence of Babylon brought a variety of responses from Judean prophets. The prophet Nahum saw glory returning to Judah. Habakkuk sees Judah needing reprimand for its faults: "Destruction and violence are before me; strife and contention arise. So the law becomes slack and justice never prevails. The wicked surround the righteous—therefore judgment comes forth perverted" (Habakkuk 1:3–4).

The prophet's response is to view Babylon as an instrument of God's will for Judah: "For I am rousing the Chaldeans, that fierce and impetuous nation, who march through the breadth of the earth to seize dwellings not their own" (Habakkuk 1:6).

While admitting that Judah needs to face judgment, Habakkuk questions God's wisdom in bringing the Babylonians to administer it. If the Judeans are not righteous, the Babylonians are even less so, and they are coming to trap the Judeans in their net like fish being dragged in from the sea.

Acknowledging that he does not understand God's will, Habakkuk stands ready to hear what God has planned. God assures Habakkuk that no matter what seems to be happening on the surface, God's ultimate plan for the Judeans who live in faithfulness will not be delayed. "For there is still a vision for the appointed time; it speaks of the end, and does not lie. If it seems to tarry, wait for it; it will surely come, it will not delay" (Habakkuk 2:3).

Those who trust in God will be fulfilled. Those who trust in themselves are sowing the seeds of their own destruction. Habakkuk's final response in faith is a vision of God as a mighty warrior who is the ultimate mover of history. Habakkuk rejoices in this vision:

> Though the fig tree does not blossom,
>   and no fruit is on the vines;
> though the produce of the olive fails
>   and the fields yield no food;
> though the flock is cut off from the fold
>   and there is no herd in the stalls,
> yet I will rejoice in the LORD;
>   I will exult in the God of my salvation.
> GOD, the Lord, is my strength;
>   he makes my feet like the feet of a deer,
>   and makes me tread upon the heights.
>   (Habakkuk 3:17–19)

CCC, 1817–21: The virtue of hope

67

The Sack of Jerusalem and the Fall of Judah

READ 2 KINGS 24–25

He [Nebuchadnezzar] burned the house of the LORD,
the king's house, and all the houses of Jerusalem.

2 KINGS 25:9

The reign of Josiah was the last golden age of Judah. Babylonia became the dominant power after defeating the Assyrians and the Egyptians at Carchemish in 605 BC. King Jehoiakim of Judah manages to hold on to his throne by bowing to Babylonia. However, he is unpopular with the people and criticized by Jeremiah for his brutality and his lavish spending on himself. "He did what was evil in the sight of the LORD, just as all his ancestors had done" (2 Kings 23:37).

The struggle for power between the Babylonians and the Egyptians is not over. The Babylonian ruler Nebuchadnezzar gathers his armies and once again tries to invade Egypt. He overextends his resources, and the Egyptians fight with fanatical fury to protect their homeland. After an indecisive battle, the

Babylonians retreat. Jehoiakim thinks that Babylon has been humbled in defeat and unwisely decides to rebel.

In 598 BC, the Babylonian armies move into Judah and besiege Jerusalem. During the siege, Jehoiakim dies. He is succeeded by his eighteen-year-old son, Jehoiachin. In the spring of 597 BC, Jerusalem is taken, the temple is looted, and the Jerusalem elite are carried off to exile in Babylon.

The final disaster happens ten years later, in 587 BC, when King Zedekiah, against the warning of the prophet Jeremiah, joins another rebellion against Babylon. Nebuchadnezzar is swift in responding. Now Jerusalem is totally demolished. The author of 2 Chronicles describes the loss of the temple: "All the vessels of the house of God, large and small, and the treasures of the house of the LORD, and the treasures of the king and of his officials, all these he brought to Babylon. They burned the house of God, broke down the wall of Jerusalem, burned all its palaces with fire, and destroyed all its precious vessels. He took into exile in Babylon those who had escaped from the sword" (2 Chronicles 36:18–20).

It is difficult to imagine how devastated the people felt after the destruction of Jerusalem and the temple. If we could imagine the simultaneous destruction of Washington DC, New York, Chicago, Los Angeles, and Vatican City in Rome, we could approach the despair the people felt. All the anchors of their physical, spiritual, and emotional life were destroyed. They faced a bleak future and were tempted to believe that God had abandoned them. "All her people groan as they search for bread; they trade their treasures for food to revive their strength. Look, O LORD, and see how worthless I have become" (Lamentations 1:11).

CCC, 2447–48: The sufferings of the poor

About: Jeremiah

Jeremiah ("the Lord exalts") lived and prophesied from approximately 627 BC—during the reign of Josiah—through the fall and devastation of Jerusalem in 587 BC. Judean leaders were unsuccessful at playing the game of international politics with Babylonia and Egypt. With the destruction of the city in 587 BC, Judah ceased to exist as an independent kingdom.

In Jeremiah 1:4–8, the prophet describes the call he received from God to prophesy to the people: "Now the word of the LORD came to me saying, 'Before I formed you in the womb I knew you, and before you were born I consecrated you; I appointed you a prophet to the nations'" (Jeremiah 1:4–5).

In Hebrew, the word translated "word" means "action" or "event." Jeremiah recounts the action of God in his life taking place even before he existed. He was chosen by God, who "knew" him. To "know" in the Hebrew means to know someone not just intellectually but in the most intimate way possible. God knew Jeremiah from the moment of his conception. God gave Jeremiah his vocation before he was born.

Jeremiah's response is a familiar one for many who have been called by God: "Then I said, 'Ah, Lord GOD! Truly I do not know how to speak, for I am only a boy.' But the LORD said to me, 'Do not say, "I am only a boy"; for you shall go to all to whom I send you, and you shall speak whatever I command you, Do not be afraid of them, for I am with you to deliver you, says the LORD'" (Jeremiah 1:6–8).

With God's mission comes his grace. "Then the LORD put out his hand and touched my mouth; and the LORD said to me, 'Now I have put my words in your mouth. See, today I appoint you over nations and over kingdoms, to pluck up and to pull down, to destroy and to overthrow, to build and to plant'" (Jeremiah 1:9–10).

CCC, 898–900; 2085: Vocation

68

Jeremiah's Temple Sermon
READ JEREMIAH 7; 26

Has this house, which is called by my name, become a
den of robbers in your sight?
JEREMIAH 7:11

Jerusalem barely survived the Assyrian invasion, but since the temple was not destroyed, many people think that God will never let it be destroyed. A saying in First Isaiah reinforces this. Isaiah prophesied that God would protect Jerusalem "like birds hovering overhead" (Isaiah 31:5).

Many see this passage as an unconditional commitment by God (an interpretation that Isaiah did not intend) to protect Jerusalem and the temple. (See also Psalms 46 and 48.) Jeremiah stands to set them straight: "Do not trust in these deceptive words: 'This is the temple of the LORD, the temple of the LORD, the temple of the LORD'" (Jeremiah 7:4).

Jeremiah teaches that the people cannot pray faithfully if they continue to oppress the immigrants, the orphans, and the widows. They have to stop shedding innocent blood (some practiced human sacrifice), and they must act justly toward one another. "Here you are, trusting in deceptive words to no avail. Will you steal, murder, commit adultery, swear falsely, make offerings to Baal, and go after other gods that you have not known, and then come and stand before me in this house, which is called by my name, and say, 'We are safe!'—only to go on doing all these abominations? Has this house, which is called by my name, become a den of robbers in your sight? You know, I too am watching, says the LORD" (Jeremiah 7:8–11).

Jeremiah reminds them of the destruction of the temple at Shiloh and tells them that their continued unfaithfulness will lead to the same result. God does not want burnt offerings and sacrifice without obedience to the covenant. "Obey my voice, and I will be your God, and you shall be my people; and walk only in the way that I command you, so that it may be well with you" (Jeremiah 7:23).

The people are angry that Jeremiah has attacked their safe worship, which does not include the responsibility of acting justly toward others. They have already killed another prophet, Uriah son of Shemaiah, for prophesying in this way. Now they almost kill Jeremiah, but Ahikam, an influential official of the temple, saves him.

CCC, 583–86: Jesus and the temple

69

Jeremiah Speaks against Jerusalem

READ JEREMIAH 28

Thus says the LORD: You have broken wooden bars
only to forge iron bars in place of them!
JEREMIAH 28:13

Throughout his ministry, Jeremiah was constantly in trouble with the political and religious authorities. One of the questions they raised was how you can tell if a message is from God. This is illustrated in the debate between Jeremiah, who speaks for the poor of Judean society, and Hananiah, who represents the religious establishment.

Hananiah proclaims that Judah has nothing to fear from Babylon, no matter what the political signs seem to show. "Thus says the LORD of hosts, the God of Israel: I have broken the yoke of the king of Babylon. Within two years I will bring back to this place all the vessels of the LORD's house, which King Nebuchadnezzar of Babylon took away from this place and carried to Babylon. I will also bring back to this place King Jeconiah son of Jehoiakim of Judah, and all the exiles from

Judah who went to Babylon, says the LORD, for I will break the yoke of the king of Babylon" (Jeremiah 28:2–4).

Wearing a wooden yoke, symbolizing the need for Judah to submit to Babylon, Jeremiah gets up and replies that he hopes that all Hananiah has said is right, but he does not think so: "But listen now to this word that I speak in your hearing and in the hearing of all the people. The prophets who preceded you and me from ancient times prophesied war, famine, and pestilence against many countries and great kingdoms. As for the prophet who prophesies peace, when the word of that prophet comes true, then it will be known that the LORD has truly sent the prophet" (Jeremiah 28:7–9).

Hananiah takes the yoke from Jeremiah's neck and breaks it, his way of claiming that Babylonian oppression has been broken. Jeremiah realizes that Hanianah's actions reflect not God's agenda but his own. Hananiah is not open to experiencing the presence of God in his life, as Jeremiah is. In breaking the wooden yoke around Jeremiah's neck, Hananiah is actually foretelling the iron yoke of Babylon that Judah will bear. Hananiah dies within a year.

Both Hananiah and Jeremiah proclaimed that they spoke in God's name. Who should the people believe? Jeremiah's answer was that a prophet who does not challenge the conscience of the nation is not a true prophet.

CCC, 61; 64: Role of prophets

70

Sorrow for the Fall of Judah
READ LAMENTATIONS 1

My eyes flow with tears;
for a comforter is far from me.
LAMENTATIONS 1:16

Judah has fallen. The leaders have been exiled; the temple has been destroyed. How can the people cope? Where is God in the midst of this tragedy?

The book of Lamentations is a short book of five chapters. Each of the first four chapters is a poem, and each line of the poem begins with a letter of the Hebrew alphabet in order. These poems provided the survivors of Judah's destruction with a way to express their grief and agony. By giving the survivors a structure for their mourning, the lament gave them the opportunity to express their feelings. This was the beginning of the healing process.

Lamentations first looks at the extent of the people's suffering. When they face the truth of their suffering, they see grief as an appropriate response.

My eyes are spent with weeping;
    my stomach churns;
my bile is poured out on the ground
    because of the destruction of my people,
because infants and babes faint
    in the streets of the city.

They cry to their mothers,
    "Where is bread and wine?"
as they faint like the wounded
    in the streets of the city,
as their life is poured out
    on their mothers' bosom.
        (Lamentations 2:11–12)

The people have willfully broken the covenant with God. Because of their sin, they see God as their enemy. On the surface, their suffering has been caused by their political enemies; at its heart, they see the action of God.

How the Lord in his anger
    has humiliated daughter Zion!
He has thrown down from heaven to earth
    the splendor of Israel;
he has not remembered his footstool
    in the day of his anger.

The Lord has destroyed without mercy
    all the dwellings of Jacob;

> in his wrath he has broken down
> > the strongholds of daughter Judah;
> he has brought down to the ground in
> > dishonor
> > the kingdom and its rulers.
> > (Lamentations 2:1–2)

This does not mean that the people thought God was unjust. God was justified because the people had rebelled against his word.

Expressing their grief and owning their guilt, the people can now hope in God's faithfulness: "The steadfast love of the LORD never ceases, his mercies never come to an end; they are new every morning; great is your faithfulness. 'The LORD is my portion,' says my soul, 'therefore I will hope in him'" (Lamentations 3:22–24).

CCC, 385–87: The reality of sin

71

Jeremiah's Message of Hope
READ JEREMIAH 29; 31

I will put my law within them, and I will write it on their hearts; and I will be their God, and they shall be my people.
JEREMIAH 31:33

Jeremiah remains in the devastated Judah. He does not support continued resistance to Babylon; those who do are quickly killed. Instead, Jeremiah counsels those in Babylon to move on with their lives: "Thus says the LORD of hosts, the God of Israel, to all the exiles whom I have sent into exile from Jerusalem to Babylon: Build houses and live in them; plant gardens and eat what they produce. Take wives and have sons and daughters; take wives for your sons, and give your daughters in marriage, that they may bear sons and daughters; multiply there, and do not decrease. But seek the welfare of the city where I have sent you into exile, and pray to the LORD on its behalf, for in its welfare you will find your welfare" (Jeremiah 29:4–7).

Jeremiah foresees the people returning to Jerusalem as a living community: "Thus says the LORD of hosts, the God of Israel: Once more they shall use these words in the land of Judah and in its towns when I restore their fortunes: 'The LORD bless you, O abode of righteousness, O holy hill!' And Judah and all its towns shall live there together, and the farmers and those who wander with their flocks. I will satisfy the weary, and all who are faint I will replenish" (Jeremiah 31:23–25).

Most important, God will re-create the people. Instead of only following the externals of the Law, forgetting its heart, the people will be open to speaking heart to heart with God.

> The days are surely coming, says the LORD, when I will make a new covenant with the house of Israel and the house of Judah. It will not be like the covenant that I made with their ancestors when I took them by the hand to bring them out of the land of Egypt—a covenant that they broke, though I was their husband, says the LORD. But this is the covenant that I will make with the house of Israel after those days, says the LORD: I will put my law within them, and I will write it on their hearts; and I will be their God, and they shall be my people. No longer shall they teach one another, or say to each other, "Know the LORD," for they shall all know me, from the least of them to the greatest, says the LORD; for I will forgive their iniquity, and remember their sin no more. (Jeremiah 31:31–34)

From the ashes of despair rises a spring of new hope.

CCC, 2562–64: The Holy Spirit and prayer

72

The Anger of Obadiah

READ OBADIAH

You should not have gloated over your brother
on the day of his misfortune.

OBADIAH 1:12

The author of Obadiah, the shortest book in the Old
Testament, wrote in white-hot anger at the kingdom of
Edom for its part in the conquest of Judah. The Edomites took
advantage of the Babylonian conquest in 587 BC to grab large
parts of southern Judah. Obadiah tells them they will be sorry.

> For the slaughter and violence done to your
>   brother Jacob,
>   shame shall cover you,
>   and you shall be cut off forever.
> On the day that you stood aside,
>   on the day that strangers carried off his
>   wealth,
> and foreigners entered his gates
>   and cast lots for Jerusalem,
>   you too were like one of them.

> But you should not have gloated over your brother
> > on the day of his misfortune;
> you should not have rejoiced over the people
> > of Judah
> on the day of their ruin;
> you should not have boasted
> > on the day of distress.
> You should not have entered the gate of my people
> > on the day of their calamity;
> you should not have joined in the gloating
> > over Judah's disaster
> on the day of his calamity;
> you should not have looted his goods
> > on the day of his calamity.
> > (Obadiah 1:10–13)

Obadiah's anger is based on Edom's long, bitter relationship with Judah. Obadiah remembers how the Edomites refused to let the Israelites pass through their territory on the journey to the Promised Land. David conquered Edom and made it part of his kingdom, but Edom managed to free itself from Judah's control.

While Obadiah predicts that Edom will suffer, he also reminds the exiles that God is the Lord of history and the One who will restore them: "Those who have been saved shall go up to Mount Zion to rule Mount Esau; and the kingdom shall be the Lord's" (Obadiah 1:21).

Sometime after the conquest of Judah, the people of Edom were forced out of their homeland by Arab tribes and moved to the Negev desert. The district would later be known as Idumea, the birthplace of Herod the Great.

About: Jews in Exile

Deportation of conquered populations was a common practice of invading armies. By uprooting peoples from their native lands, the conquering nations sought to suppress any temptation that the people might have to revolt against their new rulers. The Assyrians deported most of the people of the northern kingdom of Israel in 722 BC. Those who escaped the Assyrians took their stories south to Judah, preserving the memories of Elijah, Elisha, and Amos and the chronicles of the northern kingdom. Babylonia deported the leadership of Judah over a period of time, during its first invasion, in 597 BC, and between 586 BC and 582 BC. The reasons for the deportations were primarily political. Removing people from the land of their ancestors prevented possible future rebellion.

The Judean exiles, who now became the Jews, were taken to the city of Babylon, where they settled in villages set on ground newly reclaimed from the Euphrates River. There they were to develop the land. They did as Jeremiah had advised, building houses, establishing vineyards, and marrying to create new families.

The Jewish exiles lived in an environment soaked in Babylonian values. They could not get away from them. When Babylonian religious festivals were celebrated, the Babylonian creation story was told and its values taught. Jewish children went to Babylonian schools and learned the cuneiform script of the Babylonian language. Jewish students practiced their writing by copying the myths of Babylon. When they went home to report on what they had learned, they told the pagan myths they had learned in school. This led the priestly writers to write Genesis 1 to give the Jewish people a creation story that celebrated God's continuing love and care.

The first group of exiles was in Babylon for sixty years. The second group was there for at least forty-five years. Most of the original exiles died in Babylon. Their children never knew any other home. The temple, Jerusalem, the kingdoms of David and Solomon, and Israel and Judah became distant memories. How were they to keep their identity as God's chosen people?

Jewish settlements were also being established throughout the Mediterranean world. Egypt had a number of settlements, especially near the town of Aswan, where a Jewish military colony was employed by the Egyptians to defend their southern borders.

The experience of living in exile surrounded by alien religious values challenged the faith of the Jewish people. Jewish religious life would never again identify God's covenant and promise simply with living in Canaan. Jewish religion had to survive without the support of temple worship. The Jewish people had to develop a more personal expression of their faith. One of these developments was the synagogue—a place where the people assembled to worship God in their local communities.

73

The Call of Ezekiel

READ EZEKIEL 2–3

You shall speak my words to them,
whether they hear or refuse to hear.

EZEKIEL 2:7

Ezekiel ("God strengthens") was among the first exiles deported to Babylon, in 597 BC. He was from a priestly family and received his prophetic call in 593 BC. While in exile, he received news of what was happening in Judah. Like Jeremiah, Ezekiel saw the rulers of Judah leading the people to further destruction.

Ezekiel prophesies to the people of Judah and to those in exile. It is apparent to Ezekiel that in spite of their defeat and dislocation, the exiles have yet to repent of their sinful attitudes. "He [God] said to me, Mortal, I am sending you to the people of Israel, to a nation of rebels who have rebelled against me; they and their ancestors have transgressed against me to this very day. The descendants are impudent and stubborn. I am sending you to them, and you shall say to them, 'Thus says the Lord GOD'" (Ezekiel 2:3–4).

Like Jeremiah, Ezekiel discovers that preaching God's word is not easy. People still hope that God will somehow save the kingdom. However, God is adamant that no matter how uncomfortable it makes the people, Ezekiel must proclaim the word of judgment. "And you, O mortal, do not be afraid of them, and do not be afraid of their words, though briers and thorns surround you and you live among scorpions; do not be afraid of their words, and do not be dismayed at their looks, for they are a rebellious house. You shall speak my words to them, whether they hear or refuse to hear; for they are a rebellious house" (Ezekiel 2:6–7).

In a symbolic commitment to God's word and Ezekiel's prophetic ministry, Ezekiel eats the scroll of the word. He discovers that God's word is sweeter than honey, and it is to become the very fiber of Ezekiel's being.

CCC, 1814–16: Faith

74

Ezekiel on Individual Responsibility

READ EZEKIEL 18

The righteousness of the righteous shall be his own,
and the wickedness of the wicked shall be his own.
EZEKIEL 18:20

What does it mean for individuals to take responsibility for their actions? The people in exile recite the proverb "The parents have eaten sour grapes, and the children's teeth are set on edge" (Ezekiel 18:2), meaning that they believe they are being punished for the sins of their parents. Ezekiel replies that they have to take responsibility for themselves. Through Ezekiel, God makes it very clear that each person will be individually judged before God: "Know that all lives are mine; the life of the parent as well as the life of the child is mine: it is only the person who sins that shall die" (Ezekiel 18:4).

Ezekiel gives an example of three generations. In the first generation, the father follows God and is a model of goodness. Then the son disobeys the law, worships false idols, and persecutes the poor. In the third generation, the son, avoiding the mistakes of his father, follows the example of his grandfather. Should the son in the third generation be judged on the basis of his father's actions? Ezekiel says no! "The person who sins shall die. A child shall not suffer for the iniquity of a parent, nor a parent suffer for the iniquity of a child; the righteousness of the righteous shall be his own, and the wickedness of the wicked shall be his own" (Ezekiel 18:20).

Ezekiel further explains that even though people may follow the ways of evil for a time, they will find mercy if they convert and turn their lives to God: "None of the transgressions that they have committed shall be remembered against them; for the righteousness that they have done they shall live" (Ezekiel 18:22).

Ezekiel also cautions that good deeds cannot be stored up to somehow excuse a later evil deed: "None of the righteous deeds that they have done shall be remembered; for the treachery of which they are guilty and the sin they have committed, they shall die" (Ezekiel 18:24).

To those who would claim that God is being unfair, Ezekiel replies that, on the contrary, God is always ready to forgive. "Cast away from you all the transgressions that you have committed against me, and get yourselves a new heart and a new spirit! Why will you die, O house of Israel? For I have no pleasure in the death of anyone, says the Lord GOD. Turn, then, and live" (Ezekiel 18:31–32).

CCC, 1422–29: Penance and reconciliation

75

Creating a New People
READ EZEKIEL 36–37

I will remove from your body the heart of stone
and give you a heart of flesh.
EZEKIEL 36:26

After the fall of Jerusalem in 587 BC and the arrival in Babylon of the remainder of the exiles, Ezekiel prophesies that God will not leave the people in desolation but will come to them in love and mercy. "For thus says the Lord GOD: I myself will search for my sheep, and will seek them out. . . . I will rescue them from all the places to which they have been scattered on a day of clouds and thick darkness" (Ezekiel 34:11–12).

Ezekiel then says that the time of suffering for a repentant people is over and that God will re-create the land and bring the people home. The Promised Land will be fruitful and inhabited by God's people, as in former times (Ezekiel 36:8, 11).

Like Jeremiah, Ezekiel sees God moving to make a new people, who will have the law of God written in their hearts. "A new heart I will give you, and a new spirit I will put within you; and I will remove from your body the heart of stone and give you a heart of flesh. I will put my spirit within you, and make you follow my statutes and be careful to observe my ordinances. Then you shall live in the land that I gave to your ancestors; and you shall be my people, and I will be your God" (Ezekiel 36:26–28).

Finally, in well-known images that show God's power to create life, Ezekiel prophesies that dead Israel will come back to life.

> The hand of the Lord came upon me, and he brought me out by the spirit of the Lord and set me down in the middle of a valley; it was full of bones. He led me all around them; there were very many lying in the valley, and they were very dry. He said to me, "Mortal, can these bones live?" I answered, "O Lord God, you know." Then he said to me, "Prophesy to these bones, and say to them: O dry bones, hear the word of the Lord. Thus says the Lord God to these bones: I will cause breath to enter you, and you shall live. I will lay sinews on you, and will cause flesh to come upon you, and cover you with skin, and put breath in you, and you shall live; and you shall know that I am the Lord." (Ezekiel 37:1–6)

CCC, 798: The Holy Spirit

About: The Priestly Writers

L iving in exile in Babylon gave the people a great deal of time to think. It seemed that the superior forces of Babylon had defeated their God. How could God have let that happen? How could they keep their faith alive?

Among those taken into exile were the temple priests. These teachers had memorized the traditions of the people and also probably brought along as many texts as they could. The teaching priests were called to help the people understand the ways of God. While in Babylon, the priests continued to teach, reflect on, copy, and edit the stories they had brought with them. Following the lead of the prophets, the priests realized that covenant faith was not simply a matter of living in the Promised Land. The Promised Land was now lost. That meant that either God had abandoned the people or they had to try to understand the deeper meaning of God's covenant.

The priests saw that covenant faith meant building a religious community. True worship involved giving reverence and honor to God, who is holy. It also involved keeping the commandments and treating one another, especially the poor, with compassion. Without temple sacrifice, the religious life of the people now centered on the ritual and ethical laws of the Torah.

In this period of exile, the first edition of the Old Testament canon was collected. This included the historical books of the Old Testament (such as 1 and 2 Samuel and 1 and 2 Kings). Most of the major preexilic prophetic works were collected and edited. The books of Ezekiel and Isaiah 40–55 were written. The priestly editors emphasized the stories and teachings that spoke to their situation in exile. They wrote the first chapter of Genesis as a hymn of praise to God, whose word created and upheld the world.

Above all, the priestly writers told the people not to give up on God. The God who had created them as a covenant people was the same God who sustained them in exile and would meet them as they moved into the future.

76

The Time for Consolation

READ ISAIAH 40

Comfort, O comfort my people,
says your God.
Speak tenderly to Jerusalem.
ISAIAH 40:1–2

First Isaiah prophesied in Jerusalem during the period of the Assyrian invasion. His message was one of hope when everything seemed to go against the kingdom of Judah. A prophet in Babylon who cherished the memory of Isaiah wrote Isaiah 40–55. This prophet, called Second Isaiah, prophesied to the people in exile with words of comfort and hope.

Second Isaiah emphasized the same themes as First Isaiah. He stressed the holiness of God, who used foreign powers as his instruments to punish the chosen people but also punished those powers if they used excessive force. Second Isaiah especially emphasized that God would continue to act for his people, as he had done in the past.

The first words of Second Isaiah, also found in the introduction of Handel's *Messiah*, are words of consolation and comfort. God has sent his prophet to tell the people that the time of punishment is over.

> Comfort, O comfort my people,
>   says your God.
> Speak tenderly to Jerusalem,
>   and cry to her
> that she has served her term,
>   that her penalty is paid,
> that she has received from the LORD's hand
>   double for all her sins. (Isaiah 40:1–2)

God tells the messenger to speak tenderly to Jerusalem (in other translations, this is "to the heart of Jerusalem"). Jerusalem here means the people of God. Speaking to the heart means speaking to the center of each person, where he or she makes fundamental decisions. In saying that Jerusalem has received double for her sins, Isaiah means that the process of suffering has fulfilled its purpose of completing the process of repentance. Isaiah also implies that the pain the Jewish people have suffered is redemptive not only for the chosen people but for others as well.

Now that the process of repentance is complete, a new exodus is promised, in which Israel will be saved and other nations will know God as well.

A voice cries out:
"In the wilderness prepare the way of the
      Lord,
    make straight in the desert a highway for
      our God.
Every valley shall be lifted up,
    and every mountain and hill be made
      low;
the uneven ground shall become level,
    and the rough places a plain.
Then the glory of the Lord shall be
      revealed,
    and all people shall see it together,
    for the mouth of the Lord has spoken."
      (Isaiah 40:3–5)

CCC, 272: God's presence in powerlessness;
375: Original holiness

77

The Power of God's Word
READ ISAIAH 43; 55

My word . . .
shall not return to me empty,
but it shall accomplish that which I purpose.
ISAIAH 55:11

We can look at the circumstances in our lives in two
ways. We can examine our successes and failures, our
joys and sorrows on the surface, seeing only the immediate,
obvious effects. Or we can reflect on the inner meanings of
these events, especially our failures, and learn in the process
about our character, the meaning of true friendship, and how
God works in our lives in mysterious ways.

Second Isaiah prophesies to a people who have experienced
failure, who have lost everything but their lives, who can share
with their children only stories of the land they have left behind.
He tells them that to discover the real meaning of these events
in their lives, they have to look deeper. When they interpret the
power of God only in terms of worldly success or failure, they
are not seeing things right. They have to reinterpret what the

power of God means. God is continually present, even when everything seems to go wrong.

> A voice says, "Cry out!"
>> And I said, "What shall I cry?"
> All people are grass,
>> their constancy is like the flower of the
>>> field.
> The grass withers, the flower fades,
>> when the breath of the LORD blows
>>> upon it;
>> surely the people are grass.
> The grass withers, the flower fades;
>> but the word of our God will stand
>>> forever. (Isaiah 40:6–8)

The people experience the yearly agricultural cycle, seeing flowers bloom, wither, and die and bloom again in the spring, but this is not something that happens automatically. Second Isaiah stresses that life comes into bloom every year through the power of the word.

> For as the rain and the snow come down
>> from heaven,
>> and do not return there until they have
>>> watered the earth,
> making it bring forth and sprout,
>> giving seed to the sower and bread to the
>>> eater,

> so shall my word be that goes out from my
> mouth;
> it shall not return to me empty,
> but it shall accomplish that which I purpose,
> and succeed in the thing for which I sent it.
> (Isaiah 55:10–11)

In the same way, God will re-create the people.

> But now thus says the LORD,
> he who created you, O Jacob,
> he who formed you, O Israel:
> Do not fear, for I have redeemed you;
> I have called you by name, you are mine.
> When you pass through the waters, I will be
> with you;
> and through the rivers, they shall not
> overwhelm you;
> when you walk through fire you shall not be
> burned,
> and the flame shall not consume you.
> For I am the LORD your God,
> the Holy One of Israel, your Savior.
> (Isaiah 43:1–3)

> *CCC*, 1502: God heals the spiritually sick

About: The Rise of Persia

When the Babylonians dominated the Fertile Crescent, none of the smaller states or cities could stand up to them. But the days of Babylonian dominance were numbered. The Persian ruler Cyrus II ("the Great") was beginning to carry out his ambition to rule a great empire. Cyrus conquered the Medes around 550 BC and, moving west into present-day Turkey, attacked the kingdom of Lydia. After capturing Sardis, the capital of Lydia, he moved east into present-day Pakistan and Afghanistan. By this time, Cyrus ruled the largest empire in the ancient world, and it was only a matter of time before he attacked Babylon.

Cyrus met and defeated the Babylonian armies at Opis, on the Tigris River. The last Babylonian ruler fled for his life. Cyrus entered Babylon in 539 BC and declared that the people could continue to worship their gods. Religious tolerance was the mark of his empire. Cyrus committed no offenses against Marduk, the chief Babylonian god, and proclaimed himself the king of Babylon. He was therefore accepted by the people as Marduk's choice.

The prophet whose writings we find in Second Isaiah (Isaiah 40–55) saw the hand of God working in the success of Cyrus.

> Thus says the LORD to his anointed, to
>   Cyrus,
>   whose right hand I have grasped
>   to subdue nations before him
>   and strip kings of their robes,

to open doors before him—
   and the gates shall not be closed:
I will go before you
   and level the mountains,
I will break in pieces the doors of bronze
   and cut through the bars of iron,
I will give you the treasures of darkness
   and riches hidden in secret places,
so that you may know that it is I, the LORD,
   the God of Israel, who call you by your
     name. (Isaiah 45:1–3)

Second Isaiah's naming of Cyrus as the Lord's anointed was a revolutionary statement. It meant that God was willing to use a non-Israelite to help those in exile.

Carrying out his policy of tolerance for all religions, Cyrus freed the exiles and allowed them to return to Judah. "Thus says King Cyrus of Persia: The LORD, the God of heaven, has given me all the kingdoms of the earth, and he has charged me to build him a house at Jerusalem, which is in Judah. Whoever is among you of all his people, may the LORD his God be with him! Let him go up" (2 Chronicles 36:23).

78

A God for All the Nations

READ ISAIAH 43

Let all the nations gather together,
and let the peoples assemble.

ISAIAH 43:9

There was a long tradition in the history of the people of Israel and Judah that they were a chosen people, especially favored by God: "For you are a people holy to the LORD your God; the LORD your God has chosen you out of all the peoples on earth to be his people, his treasured possession" (Deuteronomy 7:6).

When Israel and Judah were kingdoms, this was often interpreted as meaning that God would ensure their prosperity. This interpretation was criticized by prophets like Jeremiah, who reflected the despair of Judah in defeat, beaten by more powerful enemies. "Have you completely rejected Judah? Does your heart loathe Zion? Why have you struck us down so that there is no healing for us? We look for peace, but find no good; for a time of healing, but there is terror instead" (Jeremiah 14:19).

In Second Isaiah, there is a new understanding of what it means to be God's chosen people. It is based on the realization that the people are being called to be a religious community praising the all-powerful God in their ritual and acting with compassion toward one another. In this way, the people will be a new light to the nations, attracting people to the presence of the living God in the world. "Here is my servant, whom I uphold, my chosen, in whom my soul delights; I have put my spirit upon him; he will bring forth justice to the nations" (Isaiah 42:1).

For Second Isaiah, justice, or righteousness, is God's justice, described as the bringing to earth of God's salvation. "Shower, O heavens, from above, and let the skies rain down righteousness; let the earth open, that salvation may spring up, and let it cause righteousness to sprout up also; I the LORD have created it" (Isaiah 45:8).

It is in fulfilling their vocation as witnesses to God's gracious mercy on all the world that the people will discover what it means to be the chosen servants of God. "You are my witnesses, says the LORD, and my servant whom I have chosen, so that you may know and believe me and understand that I am he. Before me no god was formed, nor shall there be any after me" (Isaiah 43:10).

79

The Suffering Servant
READ ISAIAH 52:13–53:12

He was wounded for our transgressions,
crushed for our iniquities . . .
by his bruises we are healed.
ISAIAH 53:5

The texts from Second Isaiah that had the most impact on the New Testament writers are the "suffering servant" passages found in Isaiah 52:13–53:12. These passages are usually connected with Isaiah 42:1–4, Isaiah 49:1–6, and Isaiah 50:4–9, all of which center on the theme of a servant of the Lord as the devout representative of God's caring presence.

The servant is identified with Israel (Isaiah 41:9). The reason for the servant's suffering seems to be that the people have rejected God's teaching. "I gave my back to those who struck me, and my cheeks to those who pulled out the beard; I did not hide my face from insult and spitting" (Isaiah 50:6).

Second Isaiah directs the listeners to see with eyes of faith what God sees in the servant. From the outside, the servant does not look like much. "He had no form or majesty that we should look at him, nothing in his appearance that we should desire him. He was despised and rejected by others; a man of suffering and acquainted with infirmity; and as one from whom others hide their faces he was despised, and we held him of no account" (Isaiah 53:2–3).

However, those moved to repent through the servant's quiet example are filled with his spirit of sorrow and hope.

> Surely he has borne our infirmities
> and carried our diseases;
> yet we accounted him stricken,
> struck down by God, and afflicted.
> But he was wounded for our transgressions,
> crushed for our iniquities;
> upon him was the punishment that made us whole,
> and by his bruises we are healed.
> (Isaiah 53:4–5)

Through the servant's suffering, the people will be reunited with God. "Therefore I will allot him a portion with the great, and he shall divide the spoil with the strong; because he poured out himself to death, and was numbered with the transgressors; yet he bore the sin of many, and made intercession for the transgressors" (Isaiah 53:12).

Israel's suffering and imminent restoration is more than a simple cycle of punishment and forgiveness. Through its suffering and restoration, Israel might become a means by which other nations will know God. Israel's story is a prophetic message of hope for the entire world.

CCC, 601: The atonement

About: The Return to Jerusalem

Second Isaiah's inspired insight that the Persians would act as God's instrument in freeing the people was fulfilled by Cyrus in 539 BC.

> Thus says King Cyrus of Persia: The LORD, the God of heaven, has given me all the kingdoms of the earth, and he has charged me to build him a house at Jerusalem in Judah. Any of those among you who are of his people—may their God be with them!—are now permitted to go up to Jerusalem in Judah, and rebuild the house of the LORD, the God of Israel— he is the God who is in Jerusalem; and let all survivors, in whatever place they reside, be assisted by the people of their place with silver and gold, with goods and with animals, besides freewill offerings for the house of God in Jerusalem. (Ezra 1:2–4)

Unlike the Assyrians and the Babylonians, Cyrus respected local gods and promoted local self-rule. In sending the Jews back to Canaan, Cyrus was carrying out his general policy. Cyrus not only gave the exiles permission to leave Babylon but also provided money to support the project. In addition, he allowed the returning exiles to bring back the valuable gold and silver cups and plates that the Babylonians had taken when they ransacked the temple.

Not all the exiles were ready to return, especially the many who had by now established homes in Babylon. Only a minority of the people actually made the trip. The first group returned under Sheshbazzar in about 537 BC. When they arrived at Jerusalem, they found the site of the temple in utter chaos. They started to rebuild the temple but were only able to lay its foundations.

Some twenty years later, a second group, under Zerubbabel and the priest Joshua, came to Jerusalem. The people who had inhabited the land since the fall of Jerusalem did not welcome either the earlier exiles or this group. The people of Samaria did not welcome them either, and both the Samaritans and other local groups did their best to block the rebuilding of Jerusalem's city walls and the temple. This hostility had kept the first group of returned exiles from making any meaningful progress in rebuilding the temple.

In 520 BC, the prophets Haggai and Zechariah began to insist that God was impatient for the temple to be rebuilt. The people responded with extra effort, and the temple was completed by 515 BC. But the hostility of the local inhabitants kept the returned exiles from feeling comfortable about their situation.

80

Baruch's Message to Refugees
READ BARUCH

God will give you back to me with joy and gladness forever.
BARUCH 4:23

All over the world, refugees and other displaced persons struggle to make a life for themselves in foreign lands. The United States was built by people who became displaced persons in a strange land because of economics, persecution for religious beliefs, or simply wanting to see what was over the horizon. The book of Baruch was written for people such as these.

Baruch was a disciple of Jeremiah and was probably responsible for collecting and preserving Jeremiah's writings. While the book of Baruch opens in the setting of the Babylonian exile, many scholars place its writing and its message in the postexilic age, directed to communities who had realized that they had to find their destiny outside the Promised Land. The book addressed the needs of a people who were displaced, physically and mentally. Its purpose was to help them reestablish themselves and find the right way to live in peace with God and their neighbors.

Baruch says that the people in exile will survive through their faith in the one God: "This is our God; no other can be compared to him. He found the whole way to knowledge, and gave her to his servant Jacob and to Israel, whom he loved" (Baruch 3:35–36).

Sin disrupts God's relationship with the people, bringing suffering in its wake: "Pray also for us to the Lord our God, for we have sinned against the Lord our God, and to this day the anger of the Lord and his wrath have not turned away from us" (Baruch 1:13).

The people can reconcile their relationship with God only through repentance. "Hear, O Lord, our prayer and our supplication, and for your own sake deliver us, and grant us favor in the sight of those who have carried us into exile" (Baruch 2:14).

With repentance and reconciliation comes new hope for a future of unending joy with God.

> Take courage, my children, cry to God,
>   and he will deliver you from the power
>   and hand of the enemy.
> For I have put my hope in the Everlasting to
>   save you,
>   and joy has come to me from the Holy
>   One,
> because of the mercy that will soon come to
>   you
>   from your everlasting savior.

> For I sent you out with sorrow and weeping,
>   but God will give you back to me with
>   joy and gladness forever.
>   (Baruch 4:21–23)

Baruch reminds the homeless and the displaced that whatever their situation in life, they can pray to God. If they are no longer in the Promised Land, or if they are living in times of trial, they can reflect on their memories of what God has done for them and be reminded of what God continues to do for them each day. This will be a source of hope, giving them strength to live faithfully even when the odds are against them.

CCC, 1911: The common good

81

Haggai and the Temple
READ HAGGAI

Take courage, all you people of the land,
says the LORD; work, for I am with you.
HAGGAI 2:4

An important religious event such as a retreat can be an exciting and memorable experience. The atmosphere of the retreat setting and the devotional environment it provides make us think that our lives are being changed and renewed. Then we come back to the everyday world, with its problems and distractions, and the promises we made to ourselves and to God at the retreat seem difficult to follow.

This is something like the experience of the original exiles who returned to Jerusalem. They were not welcomed in Canaan. They had to start from scratch, surrounded by enemies, and at first were not able to rebuild the temple. When the second group of exiles arrived under Zerubbabel and the high priest Joshua, a prophet named Haggai pushed to have the temple completed.

Haggai is tired of the excuses the people give for not rebuilding the temple. They say it is not the proper time and that there are too many difficulties. Haggai responds: "Is it a time for you yourselves to live in your paneled houses, while this house [the temple] lies in ruins? Now therefore thus says the Lord of hosts: Consider how you have fared. You have sown much, and harvested little; you eat, but you never have enough; you drink, but you never have your fill; you clothe yourselves, but no one is warm; and you that earn wages earn wages to put them into a bag with holes" (Haggai 1:4–6).

Haggai notes that no matter how hard the people try, they think they can't get ahead: the harvest is too small, they don't have enough to drink, and they never feel as if they have enough money.

Haggai is telling them that they do not have their priorities straight. The reason they feel so poor is that they do not honor God and do not see that everything they have is a divine blessing. Haggai promises that with the temple rebuilt, the people will be able to realize the prosperity that they hope for.

Haggai tells the Judean leaders to complete the temple and assures them of God's continuing presence. "Yet now take courage, O Zerubbabel, says the Lord; take courage, O Joshua, son of Jehozadak, the high priest; take courage, all you people of the land, says the Lord; work, for I am with you, says the Lord of hosts, according to the promise that I made you when you came out of Egypt. My spirit abides among you; do not fear" (Haggai 2:4–5).

82

Zechariah's Visions of Hope
READ ZECHARIAH 1–2

I have returned to Jerusalem with compassion;
my house shall be built in it.
ZECHARIAH 1:16

Zechariah and Haggai were colleagues in Jerusalem who had returned with the exiles from Babylon. "Now the prophets, Haggai and Zechariah son of Iddo, prophesied to the Jews who were in Judah and Jerusalem, in the name of the God of Israel who was over them" (Ezra 5:1).

Both Haggai and Zechariah proclaimed to the people that the temple must be rebuilt. As we have seen, Haggai appealed directly to the people, telling them that they did not have their priorities straight. They claimed to be poor but were more concerned with building up their own luxuries than building a fit place for God to be worshiped. Haggai emphasized the people's need to act responsibly.

Using vivid language and imagery, Zechariah emphasizes the role that God plays in the lives of the people. After the experience of the Exile and of things not automatically falling into place when they returned to Jerusalem, the people need assurance of God's care and concern for them.

First, Zechariah warns the people not to be like their ancestors, who did not heed the warnings of the prophets in the past. Now the people's ancestors and the prophets have long passed away. God's word, however, endures for the people to follow today.

Zechariah then describes a series of visions to help the people realize how God is working to direct the events of history. In his first vision, angels are riding four horses. These angels are God's messengers, roaming the world. They bring back a message of peace, the precondition for rebuilding the temple. God then promises: "Therefore, thus says the LORD, I have returned to Jerusalem with compassion; my house shall be built in it, says the LORD of hosts, and the measuring line shall be stretched out over Jerusalem. Proclaim further: Thus says the LORD of hosts: My cities shall again overflow with prosperity; the LORD will again comfort Zion and again choose Jerusalem" (Zechariah 1:16–17).

In further visions, Zechariah supports the efforts of Joshua, the high priest, and Zerubbabel, who is slated to rule the new province of Jerusalem. In the process, Zechariah inspires the imagination of the community, giving them hope that God is working for the good of the people in hidden ways.

83

Malachi's Warnings

READ MALACHI

Who can endure the day of his coming,
and who can stand when he appears?
MALACHI 3:2

Malachi ("my messenger") began prophesying in Jerusalem around 515 BC, after the temple had been rebuilt and before the coming of Ezra and Nehemiah. Zechariah's and Haggai's visions for the future were not realized as quickly as the people hoped, and they were again getting discouraged. "I have loved you, says the LORD. But you say, 'How have you loved us?'" (Malachi 1:2).

The temple has been rebuilt, although not to its former splendor, and sacrifices are being offered, but Malachi warns that the sacrifices are being abused. The sacrificial animals are not the best animals but are lame, blind, and sick. Malachi notes that the pagan peoples would not dare offer such animals to their gods. What an insult to God that his own people are willing to do so!

Worst of all, the sacrificial animals are coming from officials who have stolen them from the poor. "'What a weariness this is,' you say, and you sniff at me, says the LORD of hosts. You bring what has been taken by violence or is lame or sick, and this you bring as your offering! Shall I accept that from your hand? says the LORD. Cursed be the cheat who has a male in the flock and vows to give it, and yet sacrifices to the Lord what is blemished; for I am a great King, says the LORD of hosts, and my name is reverenced among the nations" (Malachi 1:13–14).

Malachi warns that these and other abuses will result in swift punishment from God. "Then I will draw near to you for judgment; I will be swift to bear witness against the sorcerers, against the adulterers, against those who swear falsely, against those who oppress the hired workers in their wages, the widow and the orphan, against those who thrust aside the alien, and do not fear me, says the LORD of hosts" (Malachi 3:5).

In order for the people to be faithful, they must remember the Law and God's covenant, which was made for the ages. Looking forward to a new age when God will again manifest himself, Malachi prophesies the return of Elijah to direct the people and prepare them for his coming: "Lo, I will send you the prophet Elijah before the great and terrible day of the LORD comes. He will turn the hearts of parents to their children and the hearts of children to their parents, so that I will not come and strike the land with a curse" (Malachi 4:5–6).

CCC, 2099–2100: Sacrifice

84

Ezra and the Gentile Spouses

READ EZRA 9

Do not give your daughters to their sons,
neither take their daughters for your sons.
EZRA 9:12

Abraham Lincoln once said that he thought the Bible was the most important book in the world, but he had no use for the institutional church. Many people today would agree with him. We find it easy to criticize our institutions. We criticize our schools and government agencies. We criticize the church, creating in our minds a false dichotomy between a religion of the heart and a religion of the institution. What we are slow to realize is the importance of the institution in preserving our religious heritage.

When Ezra came to Jerusalem from exile in Babylon, he found the people in a similar situation. They had built a temple in spite of great difficulties but generally disregarded the regulations about sacrifice, worship, purity, and basic Jewish customs. In addition, the Jews who had returned had married gentiles. While these marriages had been made in good faith, they represented a threat to the community, because Jewish religious practices could not be celebrated in the home. The Jewish religion as an institution was threatened.

Ezra faces the problem directly. He calls the people together and tells them how appalled he is at the situation. "When I heard this, I tore my garment and my mantle, and pulled hair from my head and beard, and sat appalled. Then all who trembled at the words of the God of Israel, because of the faithlessness of the returned exiles, gathered around me while I sat appalled until the evening sacrifice" (Ezra 9:3–4).

In his prayer in the evening sacrifice, Ezra makes clear what he thinks is required of the people. Intermarriage must cease, and the people must strive to remain within the Jewish tradition. "Therefore do not give your daughters to their sons, neither take their daughters for your sons, and never seek their peace or prosperity, so that you may be strong and eat the good of the land and leave it for an inheritance to your children forever" (Ezra 9:12).

Ezra was making a judgment about the needs of the people in his time. It contributed to a measure of hostility toward gentiles that the Bible as a whole rejects. Still, at its core, Ezra's judgment was based on the realization that the people would disintegrate if they did not practice their faith in the home— which would be impossible if the home had to support a variety of religious practices and faiths. The people would lose their sense of what it meant to be God's chosen people and to be holy and set apart as a community.

CCC, 1655–58: The family

About: Nehemiah

Nehemiah was a Jewish official who served in the court of the Persian king Artaxerxes I. He was cupbearer, meaning that he was responsible for serving food and drink at the king's table. This was a position of trust and confidence, as Nehemiah was responsible for protecting the king from assassination through poisoning. Being cupbearer also meant that he was in a position to influence Artaxerxes in matters of policy.

When Nehemiah's brother and other leaders from Jerusalem visited him, Nehemiah learned of the dire conditions in the city. "The survivors there in the province who escaped captivity are in great trouble and shame; the wall of Jerusalem is broken down, and its gates have been destroyed by fire" (Nehemiah 1:3). Heartbroken and determined to help, Nehemiah prayed to God, acknowledging the faults of the people and his own faults and asking for guidance and strength. "O Lord, let your ear be attentive to the prayer of your servant, and to the prayer of your servants who delight in revering your name. Give success to your servant today, and grant him mercy in the sight of this man!" (Nehemiah 1:11).

After persuading the king to let him return to Judah, Nehemiah was named governor and given permission to rebuild the walls of Jerusalem. When he arrived in Jerusalem, Nehemiah rallied the people and rebuilt or restored the walls in fifty-two days. However, he realized that the people were spiritually lax and must also be rebuilt. As described in chapter 85 of this book, Ezra read the Law to the people and helped them understand its demands.

Nehemiah was governor of Judah for twelve years, from 445 BC to 433 BC. He returned to the Persian court for a year or two and then was appointed governor of Judah once again. He found that the Law was still not being practiced. So he took strong action, forbidding people to do business on the Sabbath, breaking up foreign marriages, arranging financial support for the Levites, and throwing Tobiah, an Ammonite governor, out of an apartment in the temple that he had been given permission to use.

In all of this, Nehemiah showed a great sense of what it meant to live in a close relationship with God. He recognized God's power to move the Persian king for the sake of the people. He recognized that simply building external walls was not enough to save the people; they also needed religious reform. As governor, he did not take a salary but lived on his own resources. He showed what it meant to be a model servant of God.

85

Ezra and the Law
READ NEHEMIAH 8–9

*They read from the book, from the law of God, with
interpretation. . . . so that the people understood the reading.*
NEHEMIAH 8:8

When we think of the Law, we too often think of it in
a negative sense. We contrast the Old Testament as a
religion of the Law with the New Testament as a religion of
love. The implication is that the people experienced the Old
Testament Law as a burden and that religion must have been
a gloomy practice of imposed laws. However, for the returned
exiles from Babylon, learning and following the provisions of
the Law was important for their survival as a people.

This importance is highlighted in Nehemiah 8–9. "They told
the scribe Ezra to bring the book of the law of Moses, which the
LORD had given to Israel. Accordingly, the priest Ezra brought
the law before the assembly, both men and women and all who
could hear with understanding. This was on the first day of the
seventh month. He read from it facing the square before the
Water Gate from early morning until midday, in the presence
of the men and the women and those who could understand;

and the ears of all the people were attentive to the book of the law" (Nehemiah 8:1–3).

As Ezra reads the Law in the center of the square, Levites, teachers of the Law, circulate among the people to explain the meaning of what is being read. When the people hear the Law, they weep, because they have not met its demands. Ezra then tells them to go home and eat and not weep, for this is a day for rejoicing. "And all the people went their way to eat and drink and to send portions and to make great rejoicing, because they had understood the words that were declared to them" (Nehemiah 8:12).

The people then celebrate the Feast of Booths, or the Feast of Tabernacles, in which they offer the fruits of the harvest and recite the saving acts by which God delivered them from Egypt and gave them possession of the Promised Land. "And there was very great rejoicing. And day by day, from the first day to the last day, he read from the book of the law of God. They kept the festival seven days; and on the eighth day there was a solemn assembly, according to the ordinance" (Nehemiah 8:17–18).

Ezra restored the spirit of the people, helping them understand the ideal of holiness. He reemphasized the importance of the Pentateuch, the first five books of the Bible, as the norm for their daily lives. In this way, he gave them concrete direction for personal and community formation.

CCC, 1961–64: The old Law

86

Joel's Call to Repentance
READ JOEL

Return to the LORD, your God,
for he is gracious and merciful.
JOEL 2:13

Joel ("Yahweh is God") prophesied sometime after the second temple was built in Jerusalem. He was probably a temple prophet calling the people to repentance by using images from the temple ritual. His book begins with a fearsome image of a locust plague: "What the cutting locust left, the swarming locust has eaten. What the swarming locust left, the hopping locust has eaten, and what the hopping locust left, the destroying locust has eaten" (Joel 1:4).

Locusts are still a danger in northern Africa and the Near East. They come in hordes, moving across thousands of miles and stripping all vegetation of its leaves. There is no effective means to prevent their devastation. In Old Testament times, the profound destruction caused by locusts and the famine that followed made them a vivid image of God's judgment.

Joel uses this vivid imagery to call people to repentance.

Put on sackcloth and lament, you priests;
    wail, you ministers of the altar.
Come, pass the night in sackcloth,
    you ministers of my God!
Grain offering and drink offering
    are withheld from the house of your God.
Sanctify a fast,
    call a solemn assembly.
Gather the elders
    and all the inhabitants of the land
to the house of the LORD your God,
    and cry out to the LORD. (Joel 1:13–14)

Joel continues to use images of destruction to highlight the need for repentance. Fire and flame will devour the land, and God's judgment will come as a great and powerful army. In the midst of these terrible images is a call to turn to God:

Yet even now, says the LORD,
    return to me with all your heart,
with fasting, with weeping, and with
       mourning;
    rend your hearts and not your clothing.
Return to the LORD, your God,
    for he is gracious and merciful,
slow to anger, and abounding in steadfast
       love,
    and relents from punishing.
      (Joel 2:12–13)

With the people's repentance comes God's great joy in renewing the people and the land. God does not want to punish but to create. God does not want the people to suffer; he wants them to rejoice. When the people accept God's love, there will be new life. "Then afterward I will pour out my spirit on all flesh; your sons and your daughters shall prophesy, your old men shall dream dreams, and your young men shall see visions. Even on the male and female slaves, in those days, I will pour out my spirit" (Joel 2:28–29).

The apostle Peter uses these memorable verses to proclaim the coming of the Holy Spirit on Pentecost. God's promise has been fulfilled (Acts 2:17–18).

CCC, 1440–42: Penance and reconciliation

About: The Synagogue

The origins of the synagogue are not clear. The opinion of most scholars is that synagogue worship began in 586 BC, soon after the destruction of the first temple. If not then, it was soon after the Jews returned to Judea after 537 BC. In any case, synagogue worship was a revolutionary step, shifting the focus of religious practice from temple sacrifice to prayer, study, and the teaching of a rabbi, who exhorted the people to live according to the Law.

With the emergence of the synagogue, participation in worship was more widespread. There was no secret place where the priest alone would go to worship; instead, services were celebrated in full view of all the participants. Since synagogues could offer prayer and worship at the local level, they were established throughout the Mediterranean world.

The synagogue served as the center of the Jewish community. It was a place for study, for celebration of sacred meals, for judgment in civil matters, for the deposit of community funds, and for political and social gatherings. Primarily, of course, it was a center of religious activity, focused on the reading of the Torah (the first five books of the Bible) and the translating of the Torah from the Hebrew into the language of the people. The entire Torah was to be read over a period of one to three and a half years, depending on the local custom. Other religious activities at the synagogue included readings from the prophets, commentaries of the rabbis, and a sermon.

A main focus of prayer was the Shema: "Hear, O Israel: The LORD is our God, the LORD alone. You shall love the

Lord your God with all your heart, and with all your soul, and with all your might. Keep these words that I am commanding you today in your heart. Recite them to your children and talk about them when you are at home and when you are away, when you lie down and when you rise. Bind them as a sign on your hand, fix them as an emblem on your forehead, and write them on the doorposts of your house and on your gates" (Deuteronomy 6:4–9).

The existence of local synagogues was important for the early church. It was there that the earliest Christian missionaries first proclaimed that the Messiah had come in Jesus Christ. It was there that the implications of the Gospels were first understood, as they were based on the traditions of the Old Testament.

CCC, 2586; 2599: Psalms; 2701: Vocal prayer

87

Jonah's Mission to the Gentiles
READ JONAH

*Go to Nineveh, that great city, and proclaim to it
the message that I tell you.*
JONAH 3:2

How do we feel when we hear of deathbed conversions of people who have led apparently immoral lives? Does it seem as if they have stolen their way into heaven? Instead of celebrating the grace of God freely given and accepted, we can feel irrationally jealous. It just doesn't seem fair! At times, we would rather have God act more like a severe judge than a forgiving savior.

The book of Jonah was written to disparage such attitudes. Cast as a parable, it was written in Jerusalem after the exile to counter the hostility against gentiles that is apparent in the reforms of Ezra and Nehemiah.

God comes to Jonah and tells him to prophesy to Nineveh. Nineveh was destroyed a couple of centuries before, but the name symbolized the worst of the pagan world because it was the capital of Assyria. Jonah responds by trying to run away from God.

While Jonah is on board a ship, a storm arises, and the sailors conclude that Jonah is the source of the trouble. Jonah tells them to toss him into the sea. The sailors are reluctant at first but finally throw Jonah overboard, calming the sea. Jonah spends three days in the belly of a large fish. There he has a chance to reflect on and accept his mission.

Jonah goes to Nineveh and prophesies. The king of Nineveh calls for repentance; the people repent and the city is saved (Jonah 3:10).

This makes Jonah angry, and he accuses God of embarrassing him. "He prayed to the LORD and said, 'O LORD! Is not this what I said while I was still in my own country? That is why I fled to Tarshish at the beginning; for I knew that you are a gracious God and merciful, slow to anger, and abounding in steadfast love, and ready to relent from punishing. And now, O LORD, please take my life from me, for it is better for me to die than to live'" (Jonah 4:2–3).

Jonah would much prefer Nineveh unrepentant and dead.

Jonah rests, and God lets a plant grow to give him shade. The next morning, God sends a worm to eat the plant, and Jonah has to sit angrily in the sun. God's response is to say that if Jonah is upset at the loss of one plant, how much more upset would God be at the destruction of Nineveh, with all its people and animals. God is the God of all, of both the chosen people and the gentiles. Since God is the God of the gentiles, he loves them as much as he loves the chosen people.

About: Persian Influences in the Old Testament

The Jewish people lived under Persian rule from 539 BC to 332 BC. As a matter of policy, the Persians were tolerant of local customs and allowed a measure of self-rule. The Jews were even permitted to mint money for themselves.

Those exiles who wanted to go to Jerusalem were able to leave Babylon and reestablish a Jewish settlement in Canaan. The Persian government gave them financial aid and returned many of the treasures that the Babylonians had taken from the temple. Unaccustomed to such generosity, the Jewish people could not help but see the Persians as instruments of God.

Unlike the peoples in Mesopotamia and Canaan, the Persians were not Semitic. Their great prophet was Zoroaster, who lived and preached about 1000 BC. Zoroaster preached a form of belief in one god—Ahura Mazda, creator of good and evil, the just and powerful one. There were also lesser divine beings, especially a good spirit, Spenta Mainyu, and an evil one, Ahra Mainyu. These two spirits battled within the human spirit for the souls of men and women.

Lesser spirits, or "angels," also inhabited the Persian religious worldview. These represented virtues like justice, obedience, and "good empire." These angels were assistants of Ahura Mazda but were not gods with their own power.

Zoroaster also introduced the idea of moral judgment at the end of life. When those who were good died, they would receive eternal reward in heaven. Those who merited punishment would go to eternal punishment in hell, described as a lake of fire. Finally, at the end of time, there would be a final judgment of all creation. In the final judgment, Ahura Mazda would ultimately triumph over the evil of Ahra Mainyu. This would be followed by a resurrection of the dead.

If these concepts of heaven and hell, final judgment and resurrection of the dead sound familiar, it is because later Judaism would use these concepts to develop its own belief in the afterlife. These concepts would also form the background for Christian beliefs.

Persian religion also supported (in spite of Zoroaster's objections) the office of magi, or astrologers, who could read the signs of the future. The office continued into the first century, as we can see in the story of the wise men who come to pay homage to the child Jesus in the Gospel of Matthew (Matthew 2:1–12).

Persian religion survives today in India among the people called the Parsis, who continue to practice Zoroastrian rituals such as the rite of fire sacrifice, the nonburial of the dead, and the drinking of brewed *haoma* leaves as a symbol of renewed life.

88

Esther Saves the People

READ ESTHER

Perhaps you have come to royal dignity
for just such a time as this.

ESTHER 4:14

The story of Esther and her role in saving the Jewish people is a short novella full of court intrigue and set in the time of Persian domination. The main characters are the king Ahasuerus; Mordecai, a leader of the Jewish community and the guardian of Esther; and Haman, enemy of Mordecai. Finally, there is Esther, the Jewish girl who becomes the queen of Persia.

The king is upset because his wife, Vashti, will not obey his commands. He deposes her and searches for a new queen. Esther, a beautiful young Jewish girl, is found. The king falls in love and makes her his queen.

Haman is the king's chief minister. He wants to kill Mordecai because Mordecai did not give him the proper respect. To accomplish this, Haman has the king sign a decree authorizing the slaughter of all the Jews in the kingdom. Hearing of Haman's plan, Mordecai begs Esther to intercede for the Jews. He tells her that she has been chosen in this task to save her people. "For if you keep silence at such a time as this, relief and deliverance will rise for the Jews from another quarter, but you and your father's family will perish. Who knows? Perhaps you have come to royal dignity for just such a time as this" (Esther 4:14).

At the risk of her life, Esther intercedes with the king, who realizes Haman's evil intentions and orders him to be hanged. Mordecai becomes the king's chief minister. The king also gives the Jews permission to defend themselves. In self-defense, the Jews kill their enemies. They celebrate with a two-day feast called Purim, a memorial of this great victory.

The proclamation for the festival of Purim describes the story of Haman and his failure to carry out his wish to persecute the Jews. Haman cast a lot (*pur*) to determine the day of killing. Esther intervened and saved the people. "Therefore these days are called Purim, from the word Pur. Thus because of all that was written in this letter, and of what they had faced in this matter, and of what had happened to them, the Jews established and accepted as a custom for themselves and their descendants and all who joined them, that without fail they would continue to observe these two days every year, as it was written and at the time appointed" (Esther 9:26–27).

About: The Greeks

The Greek general Alexander the Great overthrew the Persian Empire in a campaign that began in 334 BC. The conquest planted Greek culture and ideas throughout Asia Minor, Mesopotamia, and Canaan. After Alexander's death, his empire became the battleground for his more talented generals, two of whom established kingdoms—in Egypt and Syria, respectively—that battled over Canaan for many decades. Like their ancestors, the Jews found themselves in between the armies of two greater powers.

Greek culture deeply influenced the Jews. The Greek world included Greek temples, gymnasiums for leisure and sport, horse-racing tracks, theaters, and youth centers to promote health and education. To get ahead in this new world, Jews had to know the Greek language, Greek philosophical concepts, and scientific concepts. Those who refused were isolated and left behind. The fortunate rich lived in idleness (and philosophical speculation), spending their time on thoughts and ideas rather than on manual labor.

Many Jews thought they could adapt to Greek ways and keep their Jewish identity. Greek ideals were popular among the young, and powerful Jewish families cooperated with the Greeks, becoming wealthy by collecting taxes for the Greek rulers. Aramaic was replaced by Greek as the language of commerce and social interaction.

Under Ptolemy II (285–246 BC), Jewish scholars began to translate the Old Testament into Greek. This eventually produced the Septuagint, the Greek translation of the Old

Testament used by the early church. Greek influence can be found in Old Testament books such as Tobit, Ecclesiasticus (or Sirach), and Wisdom. An easier flow of ideas and beliefs from Persia and the East also began to influence Jewish thought. Apocalyptic thought and language, ideas of heaven and hell, a more positive view of the afterlife—all showed up in biblical books of this period.

Greek supremacy led to severe persecution of the Jews when the Seleucid dynasty, based in Syria, overthrew the Ptolemies, who were based in Egypt, in 199 BC. The Seleucids reversed the tolerant policy of the Ptolemies and tried to force the Jewish people to adopt Greek culture and religion.

The Seleucid king Seleucus IV (187–175 BC) attempted to steal the temple treasury. His successor, Antiochus IV Epiphanes ("God made manifest"; 175–164 BC), disgraced the temple priesthood by selling the position of high priest to the highest bidder. This led to a succession of unworthy candidates. The final winner was Menelaus, who paid his bribe by giving away the gold plate from the temple treasury. Menelaus then proceeded to try to make Jerusalem over into a Greek city. He established an assembly, a citizen voting body, a gymnasium, and a school for training young men in athletics. Jews were pressured to conform to the lifestyle of the Greek-inspired world.

Faithful Jews led by the priest Mattathias and his sons Judas, Jonathan, and Simon rebelled against Menelaus. In reaction, Antiochus IV attacked Jerusalem, looted the temple, and tried to compel the Jews to give up their faith. The temple was defiled, and a statue of the Greek god Zeus was placed in the sanctuary. Jews were told to offer pigs in sacrifice and not to celebrate the Sabbath or any of their other religious festivals. Antiochus further forbade the Jews to abstain from pork and to practice the ritual of circumcision.

This challenge to the Jewish way of life led the Jews to rebel against the Seleucids. A bitter war followed, as described in 1 and 3 Maccabees. Continuing troubles with Greek and later Roman rulers caused the Jewish people to realize that their powerful enemies could not be defeated. Many Jews began to believe that God would descend with his angels to sweep these enemies away. This belief helped create a kind of literature called *apocalyptic*, of which the book of Daniel was the most influential example.

89

The Faithfulness of Tobit

> *Grant that she and I may find mercy*
> *and that we may grow old together.*
>
> TOBIT 8:7

During the postexilic period, the Jewish people came under increasing pressure to compromise with the values of the Greek-speaking world. They felt this pressure in their homeland with the persecutions of Antiochus IV. At the same time, Jewish communities were being established throughout the Mediterranean world, with large communities in Babylon and Alexandria, Egypt. How could they keep traditional family values in this strange new world?

The book of Tobit is a collection of imaginative stories that were written to address that issue. It tells the story of Tobit, a man who is poor and blinded because he fulfilled his responsibility to bury a fellow Jew who had been executed. The book of Tobit also tells the story of Tobit's son Tobias and of Tobias's marriage to his relative Sarah. The angel Raphael, disguised as Tobit's relative Azariah ("God helps"), aids Tobias.

Sarah is plagued by a demon, Asmodeus, who has killed seven of Sarah's new husbands on their wedding night.

Tobias is a man of devotion and courage. He is willing to travel dangerous lands to help find the money that his father has left in trust. He is willing to marry Sarah in spite of her tragic personal history. With the help of Raphael, Tobias defeats the demon. On his wedding night with Sarah, he shows himself to be a man of prayer, dedicating their marriage to God.

> "Blessed are you, O God of our ancestors,
>> and blessed is your name in all
>>> generations forever.
> Let the heavens and the whole creation bless
>> you forever.
> You made Adam, and for him you made his
>> wife Eve
>> as a helper and support.
> From the two of them the human race
>> has sprung.
> You said, 'It is not good that the man should
>> be alone;
>> let us make a helper for him like
>> himself.'
> I now am taking this kinswoman of mine,
>> not because of lust,
>> but with sincerity.
> Grant that she and I may find mercy
>> and that we may grow old together."

> And they both said, "Amen, Amen." Then they went to sleep for the night. (Tobit 8:5–9)

Tobias and Sarah return home, where Raphael cures Tobit's blindness. Tobias then lives a long life filled with riches, a sign of his faithfulness.

Among the themes in the book of Tobit is the importance of community for the survival of Judaism. A person's commitment to community was a measure of his or her commitment to God. It was important to bury the poor, honor one's parents, and marry within the community. Tobit's and Tobias's faithfulness to God was matched by God's faithfulness to them.

CCC, 2197–2200: Respect for parents

About: The Books of Maccabees

After the death of his father, Mattathias, Judas Maccabeus led a rebellion against the Seleucids. After much success, he was captured and executed. His brother Jonathan became the leader of the Jews and worked to complete the war Judas had begun. Jonathan was not in an easy position. Bacchides, the Greek general who had defeated and killed Judas, kept the pressure up. He recaptured Jerusalem and set up a series of forts in the surrounding territory to keep it under control. Thinking he had Judea pacified, Bacchides left for Syria for two years to rest. This gave Jonathan time to reorganize.

Hearing of Jonathan's activities in Judea, Bacchides returned with an army to take care of him. Instead, Bacchides was defeated in battle and withdrew. Judea had seven years of peace, and Jonathan set himself up as a judge. Later, he accepted the appointment of high priest.

For the next few years, Jonathan walked a tightrope between various claimants to the Seleucid throne. Each side promised him more and more if he would support its faction. Jonathan used this distraction among the rulers to firm up his control over Judea and the surrounding territories. When the current Seleucid king, Apollonius, sent an army against him, Jonathan and his brother Simon defeated it.

The balancing act continued for a total of seventeen years. In addition to the Seleucid rulers, who were trying to reassert control, Jonathan had to deal with the Ptolemies coming from

Egypt to take back the land they had lost to the Seleucids centuries before. Still, he managed to keep Judea under his rule. Jonathan was finally killed by Trypho, a Seleucid ruler who had captured him through trickery.

When he heard of Jonathan's capture, Simon, the surviving brother, became ruler of Judea. Simon led his army against Trypho, who escaped to the north to work his treachery against the Seleucid rulers. Simon found Jonathan's body and buried him with honors.

Simon completed the work of Jonathan, establishing Judea as an independent state under his family, known as the Hasmoneans, who would rule until the Romans came and conquered Judea in 63 BC.

90

The Mother and Her Sons
READ 2 MACCABEES 7

Do not fear this butcher, but prove worthy of your brothers.
2 MACCABEES 7:29

How do we determine what our priorities are in this world? Are they simply centered on our own needs? What sacrifices are we willing to make for a greater good? The author of 2 Maccabees addressed this issue when he told the story of the mother and her seven sons. The author was especially interested in exploring the meaning of suffering. He wrote that the people should not be depressed by suffering at the hands of their persecutors. Suffering should be seen as a discipline from God: "Therefore he never withdraws his mercy from us. Although he disciplines us with calamities, he does not forsake his own people" (2 Maccabees 6:16).

The mother and her sons are taken prisoner by the Seleucids and brought before the king. They are tortured in an effort to make them eat pork, an action that would break the Jewish covenant. The oldest son refuses and says that death would be preferable to violating Jewish tradition. He is tortured again until he dies. Watching him die, his mother and the rest of his family encourage him, saying, "The Lord God is watching over us and in truth has compassion on us, as Moses declared in his song that bore witness against the people to their faces, when he said, 'And he will have compassion on his servants'" (2 Maccabees 7:6).

Each son is given the opportunity to deny his faith. Each refuses. Each son also speaks in hope, for they believe not only in the dignity of a faithful death but also in the resurrection. This belief in the resurrection was a new insight for the Jewish people about God's care for them beyond life on earth. Therefore, the second son can tell the Seleucid ruler in confidence, "You accursed wretch, you dismiss us from this present life, but the King of the universe will raise us up to an everlasting renewal of life, because we have died for his laws" (2 Maccabees 7:9).

The ruler is more and more astonished at the courage of the young men. When he comes to the last son, the ruler prevails on the mother to plead for her son's life, promising not only freedom but riches as well. The mother tells her son, "Do not fear this butcher, but prove worthy of your brothers. Accept death, so that in God's mercy I may get you back again along with your brothers" (2 Maccabees 7:29).

The courage of the youngest son does not fail. Enraged and exasperated, the ruler puts him to death. Finally, the mother is also killed.

CCC, 272–74: The meaning of suffering

About: The Romans

The Romans are first mentioned in the Bible in 1 Maccabees 8, where Judas Maccabeus hears of them and their strength and signs a treaty with them. Later, in 1 Maccabees 15, we read of Rome's mediation between the Jews and the court of King Ptolemy. From a distance, Rome looked like a helpful partner.

Things changed when Roman armies under Pompey came marching through Jerusalem in 63 BC. The Hasmonean kings, the descendants of the Maccabees, had become corrupt. The Romans quickly deposed them and eventually gave the kingdom of Judea to Herod the Great (73 BC–AD 4).

This was the Roman way, to rule with the help of men chosen from the local aristocracy. Rome found it convenient to have these men in place—or to appoint them, in the case of Herod—because it did not have the administrative staff in place to take direct control. The local ruler stayed in the favor of the Roman authorities by giving them generous gifts and bribes. Eventually, the local provinces were directly ruled by Rome, as Judea was under the Roman procurators.

Rome wanted two things, the maintenance of law and order and the collection of taxes. There were taxes on the land, on the people who worked the land, on all trade goods that moved from one province to another. Inheritances, all sales to local markets, and anything else Rome could think of were taxed. In the early years, Rome used local tax farmers to gather taxes. The tax farmer paid Rome a negotiated sum for a district. In return, Rome gave the tax farmer the legal right to squeeze from the district as much revenue as he could, with the power of the

Roman state to back him up. The profits for the tax farmer were enormous. Augustus Caesar (63 BC–AD 14) abolished the system. The tax collectors, or publicans, in the Gospels collected directly for the government. They were just as hated for working for the occupying powers.

Rome generally stayed out of religious issues. They did demand that local religious activities include an offering to the emperor as divine. In the case of the Jews, however, this requirement was modified to praying to God for the emperor.

The Jews hated Roman domination and rebelled against Rome in AD 66–70, and later in AD 132–35. Each time the rebellion was totally suppressed by the indomitable Roman armies. Jerusalem and the temple were destroyed in AD 70. The scattered Jewish people were no longer a religious community that offered animal sacrifices. A new form of Judaism had to rise from the ashes.

91

Daniel the Wise Hero
READ DANIEL 6

My God sent his angel and shut the lions' mouths
so that they would not hurt me.
DANIEL 6:22

The book of Daniel was written around 167 BC, while the Seleucid ruler Antiochus IV Epiphanes (175–164 BC) was persecuting the Jews. The stories in Daniel do not directly describe what happened in the time of Antiochus's persecution; they are set in the time of the last days of the Babylonian Empire and the reign of Darius, the Persian king. Daniel was written to strengthen the faith of the people, who were suffering from Antiochus's persecution. The writer used the story of the fall of Babylon as a code to give his people hope in their present suffering.

Daniel was apparently an actual person, but we know very little about him. He was considered a heroic figure in Jewish tradition (see Ezekiel 28:1–3), and his name was used to give the book credibility. The book of Daniel has two parts. The first part takes place in Babylon under Nebuchadnezzar and later under Darius, the Persian king.

Chapter 6 in the book of Daniel shows him to be a man who is faithful in spite of persecution. The story is set in the reign of Darius. Daniel is an excellent administrator of the kingdom and is given total authority. This makes the other Persian administrators jealous. They immediately try to discredit Daniel, but they fail. They finally plot to have Daniel killed. The conspirators go to King Darius and flatter him. They tell him that since he is the most powerful of rulers, no one should pray to any other god or man for thirty days. The king, taken in by their overblown compliments, signs the declaration.

Darius's decree is unjust, but he cannot revoke it. The writer uses Daniel's predicament to comment on the situation faced by the Jews in the reign of Antiochus IV, who forbade the Jews to practice their religion. Daniel, fully aware of the consequences of his actions, continues to pray to God. He does so at an open window, and his enemies see him and report him to Darius. Darius now realizes that he has been trapped by his pride, and Daniel must face punishment for his civil disobedience. Daniel is thrown in with the lions.

Darius is grief-stricken but is helpless because of his own unjust decree. He spends a sleepless night, even praying to God for Daniel's safety. In the morning, Darius discovers that Daniel is alive. An angel came to close the mouth of the lions.

Darius is happy that he still has his most faithful servant. Angry with the conspirators, he has them and their families thrown to the lions, which quickly devour them.

Mattathias, the father of the Maccabeus brothers, encouraged his sons to fight Antiochus and the Seleucid rulers with this story: "Daniel, because of his innocence, was delivered from the mouth of the lions. And so observe, from generation to generation, that none of those who put their trust in [God] will lack strength" (1 Maccabees 2:60–61).

About: The Pharisees

The Jewish people responded to Greek thinking and influence on society in Canaan in a number of ways; the Pharisees illustrate one of these. The Pharisees are thought to have originated between 200 BC and 100 BC, when Greek influence was at its highest. The term *Pharisees* probably means "the separate ones." This refers to their desire to establish a distinct form of Jewish piety that could help preserve Jewish identity.

The Pharisees were mostly a lay movement within Judaism. They struggled to oppose what they saw as Jewish people becoming too relaxed in the observance of the Law. As a movement of ordinary people, the Pharisees also opposed corruption in the Jewish aristocracy.

The principal source of information about the Pharisees is the Jewish historian Josephus (AD 37–c. 100). According to Josephus, the Pharisees were influential among the people because of their accurate interpretation of the Law. They lived simply and sought to live in harmony with others. They taught that the people had free will and would be responsible for how their souls survived after death. Unlike the Sadducees, the Pharisees believed in the resurrection of the soul.

It is not known how a person became a Pharisee. What is known is that a Pharisee devoted himself to living a faithful life as a Jew. The Pharisees emphasized ritual purity, offerings of food, and observance of the Sabbath. The people admired them because their political and social views corresponded to what the people believed. Since the Pharisees were learned in the Law, people asked them for their opinion, thus giving them political influence. Because of this, they aroused opposition by their enemies, who recognized their impact on the local scene.

After the fall of Jerusalem and the destruction of the temple in AD 70, Jewish religion was in turmoil. The religion had to be rebuilt on the basis of the written word of God in Scripture. Scholars believe that Jewish scholars of the time—many, if not most, of them Pharisees—met in the small town of Jamnia around the year AD 90 to help create the Jewish canon of Scripture and to establish Judaism as a religion of ethical service to God.

CCC, 575–76: Jesus and the Pharisees

About: The Psalms

The book of Psalms, or the Psalter, is a collection of 150 prayer-poems. Many of the Psalms are credited to King David, who was a great poet and singer. The Psalms are songs of many types that reflect the depth of Israel's relationship with God.

The Psalter is made up of five distinct collections of psalms. The first collection, Psalms 1–41, is an early collection of hymns attributed to David. Psalms 42–72 is a collection from the northern tribes. Psalms 73–89 is a collection from the temple singers. Psalms 90–106 is from a royal collection that is believed to have originated with the New Year's festivals. Finally, Psalms 107–150 is a second and expanded collection attributed to David.

The Psalms offer a variety of prayer forms. There are hymns of praise, hymns of thanksgiving, individual laments, and community laments.

The Psalms were prayed primarily in public worship in the temple. Royal psalms honor either God as king or the king on earth as God's deputy. Psalms 113–118 were probably sung during the killing of the lambs for Passover. Psalms 81 and 106 emphasized the people's repentance after a long period of unfaithfulness. Psalms 120–134 were prayed during pilgrimages.

As confessions of faith, the psalms speak to ordinary, concrete experiences. These were both positive and negative. As such, they express a variety of human emotions, including wonder, joy, confidence, thanksgiving, sorrow, despair, and fear.

The psalmists were not afraid to express their anger and rage, even toward God. They also expressed frustration, resentment, and desire for revenge. This blatant and honest expression of feelings can sound irreverent to us. However, it must be remembered that these are prayers to God that he will answer in his own way.

The Psalms were the prayer of Jesus and his family. They were also the prayer of the early church. By the third century, the Psalter became *the* book of songs for Christian worship. Throughout the Middle Ages, the Psalms were sung morning and evening in the cathedral churches. In the monasteries, the Psalms were adopted for morning and evening prayer and for special hours during the day.

The Psalms remain the prayer of the church today. We read them in the light of the mystery of Christ. They show us the authentic prayer life of the people of the Old Testament and continue to inspire us today in the daily reading of the Divine Office of the church.

CCC, 2585–89: The Psalms

92

Human Dignity
READ PSALM 8

Yet you have made them a little lower than God.
PSALM 8:5

What does it mean to be human? Does it mean following our emotions, or setting ourselves apart by the money we make or the clothes we wear? Is our goal in life to be "self-made," owing nothing to anyone? It is easy to make idols of ourselves, putting ourselves before God, family, and neighbor. The biblical tradition makes it clear that these attitudes keep us from God and from becoming the best versions of who we are called to be.

Psalm 8 is a song of wonder praising God and human dignity. The psalmist begins by singing of the majesty of God, whose glory is reflected in the stars. In the cultures that surrounded the Jewish people, the stars and the heavens were worshiped as gods. The psalmist clearly wants to say that the stars are not to be worshiped. They are but a sign of the abiding creative presence of God, who keeps them in existence.

We can be amazed at God's power in the stars. That same power enlivens us. "When I look at your heavens, the work of your fingers, the moon and the stars that you have established; what are human beings that you are mindful of them, mortals that you care for them?" (Psalm 8:3–4).

Next to the stars, human beings can seem small. We are fragile, short-lived, and ordinary. Yet God remembers us and comes to save us. "Yet you have made them a little lower than God, and crowned them with glory and honor. You have given them dominion over the works of your hands; you have put all things under their feet" (Psalm 8:5–6).

What a noble calling we are given! We are called to be stewards, under God, of all creation. The psalmist uses the same words by which a king is crowned to show that every man and woman is given the same royal vocation.

CCC, 1701–9: Man in the image of God

93

A Song of Repentance

READ PSALM 51

The sacrifice acceptable to God is a broken spirit;
a broken and contrite heart.

PSALM 51:17

Our culture has little sense of sin and the necessity of forgiveness. When people make sinful decisions and discover that they have made a mess of their lives, hopelessness is often the only result. The rate of suicide among the young, and the ease with which people hurt, even kill, one another, are part of the blindness created by sin. If we don't take responsibility for personal sin, we cannot ask for forgiveness, much less accept it.

Psalm 51 is attributed to David as a response to Nathan's fiery critique of his relationship with Bathsheba, but it was actually composed later in the period after the Jewish people returned from exile in Babylon. It is a deep reflection on human sinfulness and the need for repentance. It begins with a call to God for mercy: "Have mercy on me, O God, according to your steadfast love; according to your abundant mercy blot out my transgressions" (Psalm 51:1).

The psalmist admits that he has sinned. He asks God to be merciful and to forgive. He asks God to show his "steadfast love"; in other words, he asks God to remember the bond of the covenant, God's total commitment to the people.

In the middle verses, the psalmist describes the depths of his sin. His sin is ever before him. He has done evil in God's sight. God is right to pass judgment. The psalmist was born guilty. It is important to note in this context the story of David and Bathsheba. David had Uriah, Bathsheba's husband, killed so that David could take her. When we sin against one another, we sin against God.

The psalmist prays to God to "create in me a clean heart" (Psalm 51:10). Sin is a matter of the heart, where decisions are made for our basic direction in life. The Hebrew word *bara*, "to create," is used only of God. Only when we are open to God's creative action can we make the fundamental choice to renew our lives.

And how do we approach God in prayer? "The sacrifice acceptable to God is a broken spirit; a broken and contrite heart, O God, you will not despise" (Psalm 51:17).

God wants us to return. Our own pride, our unwillingness to let God's steadfast love and gracious mercy work in our hearts, gets in the way. If we hold on to human pride too tightly, we make no room for God's miracles to happen.

CCC, 1430–33: Repentance of the heart

94

The Lord Is My Shepherd

READ PSALM 23

Even though I walk through the darkest valley,
I fear no evil.

PSALM 23:4

Psalm 23 is easily the most familiar of all the psalms. The images of God as the shepherd and of green pastures, quietly flowing waters, and a banquet with an overflowing cup all seem to picture a quiet, peaceful day. Coupled with Christian images of Jesus tenderly holding a small lamb in his arms, the images in this psalm give the impression that all is right in the world with no effort at all.

The life of a shepherd was not an easy one. When Jacob was settling his accounts with Laban, he described the work he had done for twenty years. He had protected the sheep and had gone hungry rather than eating the rams. When wild animals ate the sheep or the lambs, Jacob bore the losses himself. "It was like this with me: by day the heat consumed me, and the cold by night, and my sleep fled from my eyes" (Genesis 31:40).

David also remembered how hard it was to be a shepherd. "Your servant used to keep sheep for his father; and whenever a lion or a bear came, and took a lamb from the flock, I went after it and struck it down, rescuing the lamb from its mouth; and if it turned against me, I would catch it by the jaw, strike it down, and kill it" (1 Samuel 17:34–35).

A shepherd had to be brave, steadfast, and caring—not like the hireling that Jesus criticizes for running away from danger (John 10:12). In Psalm 23, we pray: "Even though I walk through the darkest valley, I fear no evil; for you are with me; your rod and your staff—they comfort me" (Psalm 23:4).

The dark valley does not go away in this life. We are constantly surrounded by pitfalls, disappointments, and failures. The wolves are always at the door, ready to devour anyone who walks blindly into unstable situations. We would like to think that we are smarter than sheep. However, a quick review of the daily paper or the evening news reveals that people are certainly capable of making bad decisions and finding themselves in situations where the rod and staff of God would be of great help.

The images of the psalm tell us that God is here for us, through the heat of day and the cold of night, ever watchful while we sleep.

CCC, 553; 754: Our shepherd the church

95

Does God Forsake Us?
READ PSALM 22

My God, my God, why have you forsaken me?
PSALM 22:1

At times in our lives we feel alone and friendless. Everything we do seems to go wrong; everything we say is misunderstood. The world seems especially uncaring, and we wonder if God is even listening.

It seems that when Jesus was on the cross, he felt the same way. According to Mark 15:34, he cried in the midst of his agony: "My God, my God, why have you forsaken me?" These words are familiar to every Christian who listens with attention to the story of the Passion. Psalm 22 is quoted thirteen times in the New Testament and nine times in the Passion story.

Psalm 22 is a profound cry to God from the depths of pain. It can be the suffering of a person who is dying and feels abandoned by friends and family. Even before he dies, they gather to divide his property: "They divide my clothes among themselves, and for my clothing they cast lots" (Psalm 22:18).

This psalm could have been sung by someone who was on the road from Jerusalem to Babylon, facing a future without the temple and without his family. It could be sung by any one of us at any time in our lives—when someone in our family loses a job, or a couple we love gets divorced, or we ourselves fail at something.

The psalmist does not attack anyone and does not say that the world is unfair. He only asks God to listen. God has answered the cry of the people in the past; all the psalmist asks is that God hear his cry today. Vividly he describes his strength melting away.

In the midst of his suffering comes the certainty he is asking for. God lives in the assembly, in the words of praise proclaimed by the congregation. In them, the psalmist hears the God who acts. "For he did not despise or abhor the affliction of the afflicted; he did not hide his face from me, but heard when I cried to him" (Psalm 22:24).

From the depths of his suffering, the psalmist raises his voice to proclaim not only the God who saves him, but also the God whose grace is extended to all. "All the ends of the earth shall remember and turn to the LORD; and all the families of the nations shall worship before him" (Psalm 22:27).

CCC, 616–18: Jesus' sacrifice on the cross

96

Job and His Friends

READ JOB 20–21

How then will you comfort me with empty nothings?

JOB 21:34

We all suffer in many ways. We face disappointments in school, in work, in our families. We experience tragedy with the loss of people we love. We suffer through our own mistakes and through the actions of others. Often when we suffer, people try to help us by uttering clichés like "God knows best" and "Everything will work out for the best." Instead of bringing healing to our pain, these can increase our confusion and misery.

The author of Job examines such a situation. Job's friends Eliphaz, Bildad, Zophar, and Elihu arrive to console Job for his losses. Job is in misery and expresses his pain honestly: he never blames God, but he wishes that he had never been born. Job's friends respond that his suffering must be punishment for his sin and that he should repent. (God, however, has already declared Job blameless.) They say that God has been lenient with Job. Job responds that he is a laughingstock.

Job's friends claim that if he does not accept their interpretation of what God wants, Job is undermining religion. Job reaffirms his innocence and continues to lament. Job's friends say that God punishes the wicked and that wickedness receives its just punishment. Job replies that many of the wicked receive no punishment; indeed, "they spend their days in prosperity, and in peace they go down to Sheol" (Job 21:13).

When Job's friends tell Job that he is refusing to admit his own wickedness, Job replies that his complaint is bitter: he has not made the violence that stalks the earth. Job's friends ask how anyone can stand in a right relationship with God. Job replies that God's ways are a mystery no one can fathom.

What is fascinating about this dialogue is that Job's friends seem so sure that they know the answers to Job's dilemma. They do not for an instant consider Job's side of the story or ask questions of either Job or God. Without questioning or listening hearts, they cannot begin their own journey into the heart of God.

CCC, 2634–36: Prayer of intercession

97

Job Speaks to God

READ JOB 40; 42

I had heard of you by the hearing of the ear,
but now my eye sees you.

JOB 42:5

It is difficult for us to be honest with God. This is especially true when we are angry, disappointed, or deeply hurt. Somehow, we don't think that God will understand. We act as if God cannot take it. We pretend that we can hide our true feelings from God with dull prayers. When we hide behind clichés, as Job's friends do, a true relationship with God is impossible. This is not because of God's inability to understand; it is because of our unwillingness to be honest.

Job is seeking a true relationship with God. Starting in Job 31, he complains to God about the ways he has suffered. God has already declared Job blameless (Job 1:8), so his complaint makes some sense. Job describes all of his family and social obligations and how he has met every need with generosity. If there is anyone who accuses him of wrongdoing, let him step forward.

After his complaint, Job must listen to Elihu's defense of God. Elihu says that Job is not righteous, that God is good, and that God is total majesty. Job must consider the wonders of God and admit to his guilt.

God responds with a long description of the expanse and depth of creation. God is a God of life, of change. The abundance of images overflowing with life that God presents to Job humbles him.

> I know that you can do all things,
>> and that no purpose of yours can be
>> thwarted.
> "Who is this that hides counsel without
>> knowledge?"
> Therefore I have uttered what I did not
>> understand,
>> things too wonderful for me, which I did
>> not know.
> "Hear, and I will speak;
>> I will question you, and you declare to
>> me."
> I had heard of you by the hearing of the ear,
>> but now my eye sees you;
> therefore I despise myself,
>> and repent in dust and ashes.
>> (Job 42:2–6)

The writer of Job does not supply easy answers to Job's questions. He describes the fruitfulness of God's activity in the world, and Job is ultimately left speechless and contemplative. However, Job is assured that his suffering is not punishment for sin.

God also judges Job's friends for their easy answers. They have not spoken what is right, and Job has. They need Job's intercession in order to be reconciled to God.

The book of Job ends with God rewarding him with riches double what he owned before. He has new sons and daughters, lives to a serene old age, and dies in peace. The writer of Job does not say that he knows why suffering exists. He knows that the simple answers will not do and that suffering can have some deeper purpose, but he doesn't know what it is.

CCC, 164–65: Witnesses of faith

About: Proverbs and the Song of Songs

The book of Proverbs and the Song of Songs are classified among the wisdom literature. Both are rooted in Israel's daily experience of a practical faith. Both show an optimistic point of view.

Proverbs is a collection of wise sayings from different eras and different cultures that was probably edited in its final form after the Exile. Those who put it together wanted to include the wisdom of all peoples within Israel's faith. The dominant point of view maintains that the key to right living is fear of the Lord—meaning proper reverence and worship of Israel's God—and it suggests that obedience to the Law is the way to wisdom. However, the collection includes many proverbs giving practical and secular advice. Scholars have shown that many proverbs originated with the pagan peoples that shared the neighborhood with the Jews.

The Song of Songs is a collection of Hebrew love poetry. The eight chapters of Song of Songs are arranged to suggest a dialogue between a young lover and his bride, but the poems are actually drawn from different periods in Israel's history. The literary unity of the book is more apparent than real.

The Song of Songs rejoices in passionate love. The poems are especially notable for their frank celebration of sexual love between man and woman. They have always been interpreted allegorically. The Jewish rabbis who admitted them into the sacred canon of Scripture in the second century AD believed that they described Yahweh's love for Israel. The church has viewed the Songs of Songs in a similar fashion, as an allegory of Christ's love for the church. Over the centuries, the Song of Songs has been a rich source of reflection and imagery for mystical spirituality.

CCC, 303: God's love is immediate and practical

98

Ecclesiastes on Vanity
READ ECCLESIASTES 1–3

What do people gain from all the toil
at which they toil under the sun?
ECCLESIASTES 1:3

The writer of Ecclesiastes (also called Qoheleth, or "one who calls the assembly together") would be interested in the messages that flood the media about the "good life." We see images of people moving from success to success, living in prosperity in sprawling homes and driving fast cars. In response to all these images of the "good life," he would say:

> Vanity of vanities, says the Teacher,
>   vanity of vanities! All is vanity.
> What do people gain from all the toil
>   at which they toil under the sun? . . .
> All things are wearisome;
>   more than one can express;
> the eye is not satisfied with seeing,
>   or the ear filled with hearing.

> What has been is what will be,
> > and what has been done is what will be
> > > done;
> there is nothing new under the sun.
> > Is there a thing of which it is said,
> "See, this is new"?
> It has already been,
> > in the ages before us.
> > > (Ecclesiastes 1:2–3, 8–10)

Our culture says that it is good to be rich, powerful, and famous; that it is good to plan and create large projects, get as much money as you can, and do whatever pleases you. But is this what makes a person happy and secure? Is this how a person finds fulfillment in life? Ecclesiastes says that all of this is vanity and emptiness, creating what the poet T. S. Eliot calls "hollow men."

And while all this is going on, the universe does not change. It continues with boring repetition:

> A generation goes, and a generation comes,
> > but the earth remains forever.
> The sun rises and the sun goes down,
> > and hurries to the place where it rises.
> The wind blows to the south,
> > and goes around to the north;
> round and round goes the wind,
> > and on its circuits the wind returns.
> All streams run to the sea,
> > but the sea is not full;

> to the place where the streams flow,
>> there they continue to flow.
>>> (Ecclesiastes 1:4–7)

Instead of seeing this cycle of events as the completion of all things, Ecclesiastes sees all the work of the forces of nature as leading to nothing. The earth goes through its orbit every year, and nothing changes. All of our plans and accomplishments are irrelevant to an uncaring universe. We need to see the world for what it is. We need to practice detachment from all that the world offers. The world just goes round and round and can never be a source of permanent happiness. Instead we recognize that all we have is a gift from God.

CCC, 2544–47: Poverty of heart

About: Jewish Life in Alexandria

The Egyptian city of Alexandria, founded in 332 BC by Alexander the Great, became one of the largest cities of the Hellenistic world. It was a major shipping center with a world-renowned 445-foot-tall lighthouse. It was known for its four-hundred-thousand-volume library and museum, which was the center of the intellectual and cultural life of the Mediterranean world.

Alexandria's population grew to nearly one million and included the largest Jewish community outside of Canaan. The Jews who lived there had to learn the Greek language and deal with issues raised by Greek culture. They formed their own organizations to support their economic and educational rights and integrated many Greek points of view into their tradition. In Alexandria, the Hebrew Bible was translated into the Greek, in an edition known as the Septuagint, which would be used by the first Christians, and Wisdom of Solomon and possibly two more books of Maccabees were written in Greek.

The Jews, Egyptians, and Greeks in Alexandria did not get along. This created tensions that came to a head in 24 BC when the Roman emperor Augustus instituted a poll tax. The Greek inhabitants of the city were exempt from the tax, Greek-speaking inhabitants who were not Greek paid a lower tax, and Egyptians paid the full tax. When the Jews attempted to establish Greek citizenship so as not to pay the tax, the Greeks angrily opposed them.

These tensions erupted into bloody riots between the Jews and the Greeks. The Greeks instituted pogroms, vicious attacks on the Jewish community that resulted in the destruction of life and property. Probably for the first time in their history, the Jews were forced to live in a ghetto. The violence ended after AD 41 when the Roman emperor Claudius proclaimed a decree giving religious liberty to the Jews in Alexandria and throughout the empire. However, Jews were ordered not to apply for Greek citizenship and were not given opportunities for education and economic advancement. This eventually led to further riots and the absolute destruction of the Jewish community in Alexandria in AD 115–17.

The Jewish community in Alexandria had to face the hostility and injustice of the Egyptian and Greek communities and the surrounding influence of the many and various pagan cults and idols. The Wisdom of Solomon was one response to these pressures.

CCC, 839–40: The church and the Jewish people

99

The Meaning of a Good Life

READ WISDOM 3–4

The souls of the righteous are in the hand of God.
WISDOM 3:1

How can we tell if we are living a fulfilling life? When an older person dies surrounded by family and friends, there is sorrow, but there is also a sense that this person led a complete life. When a younger person dies, by accident, from cancer, or through abuse of drugs, there is a sense of lost potential, of incompleteness.

The writer of the Wisdom of Solomon addressed these and other issues. He wrote to make us think. For instance, a long life was usually seen in the Old Testament as a sign of God's blessing. The writer of Wisdom challenges this stereotype by saying of those who do not seek God, "Even if they live long they will be held of no account, and finally their old age will be without honor" (Wisdom 3:17).

Having many children was also a sign of blessing. But if these children are not raised correctly, they will also be lost. "The branches will be broken off before they come to maturity, and their fruit will be useless, not ripe enough to eat, and good for nothing" (Wisdom 4:5).

The basic point that the author of Wisdom makes for his listeners is that a life can be a failure in an earthly sense and still be successful before God. Childlessness, for example, was seen in the other texts of the Old Testament as a curse. On the contrary, the Wisdom writer says, "Blessed is the barren woman who is undefiled, who has not entered into a sinful union; she will have fruit when God examines souls" (Wisdom 3:13).

The writer continues, "Better than this [having children who will be lost] is childlessness with virtue, for in the memory of virtue is immortality, because it is known both by God and by mortals" (Wisdom 4:1).

Regarding the tragedy of the good person who dies young, Wisdom writes, "There were some who pleased God and were loved by him, and while living among sinners were taken up. They were caught up so that evil might not change their understanding or guile deceive their souls. . . . Being perfected in a short time, they fulfilled long years; for their souls were pleasing to the Lord, therefore he took them quickly from the midst of wickedness" (Wisdom 4:10–11, 13–14).

CCC, 1805–9: The cardinal virtues

100

The Misuse of the Tongue
Read Sirach 19–20

Have you heard something? Let it die with you.
SIRACH 19:10

Nothing destroys relationships or someone's self-esteem quicker than thoughtless conversation and gossip. People can destroy one another through spiteful words, true or untrue. One way to avoid the problems that come from speaking too freely about another's business is to keep quiet about it, no matter how strong the temptation is to speak. The writer of the book of Sirach understands this problem and says that keeping quiet will not kill anyone.

> Never repeat a conversation,
>   and you will lose nothing at all.
> With friend or foe do not report it,
>   and unless it would be a sin for you, do
>   not reveal it;

> for someone may have heard you and
>   watched you,
>   and in time will hate you.
> Have you heard something? Let it die with
>   you.
>   Be brave, it will not make you burst!
>   (Sirach 19:7–10)

The worst temptation a person has is to gossip about what he or she has heard. Once gossip is in the air, it cannot be reeled back in. "Like an arrow stuck in a person's thigh, so is gossip inside a fool" (Sirach 19:12).

Sirach condemns gossips, especially people who lie to hurt other people. "Curse the gossips and the double-tongued, for they destroy the peace of many. . . . Slander has driven virtuous women from their homes, and deprived them of the fruit of their toil. Those who pay heed to slander will not find rest, nor will they settle down in peace" (Sirach 28:13, 15–16).

Finally, if we betray our friends with a loose tongue, we can lose them forever.

> Whoever betrays secrets destroys confidence,
>   and will never find a congenial friend. . . .
> For as a person destroys his enemy,
>   so you have destroyed the friendship of
>   your neighbor. . . .
> Do not go after him, for he is too far off,
>   and has escaped like a gazelle from a
>   snare.

> For a wound may be bandaged,
>> and there is reconciliation after abuse,
>> but whoever has betrayed secrets is
>>> without hope.
>>> (Sirach 27:16, 18, 20–21)

When we have broken trust with others, we have also broken trust with God. We can overcome our smug pride only by accepting the grace of honest repentance that God continually offers. Then we can take the necessary steps to restore our relationship with God and with those we have harmed.

CCC, 1853: Types of sins; 2475–87: Offenses against truth

GLOSSARY

angel: A spiritual being ("messenger") who acts under God's command to deliver God's messages. An angel can be called to help those who are chosen for special tasks or to lead the battle against God's enemies.

apocalyptic literature: From the Greek *apokalypsis*, meaning "revelation," a type of literature in which the writer is said to receive a revelation through an angel that shows God's future intervention on behalf of the people. These works were written as messages of comfort for the people at a time when they lived under persecution.

Ark of the Covenant: The portable shrine that carries the tablets inscribed with the Ten Commandments. It was seen as a direct manifestation of God and a focal point for divine power. During the Babylonian conquest of Jerusalem in 587 BC, it was either captured or destroyed.

Asherah: A Canaanite goddess who is the consort of Baal. Worship of Asherah was especially promoted by Ahab's wife, Jezebel, making her the special enemy of Elijah.

atonement: The means by which the people are able to remove the barriers between themselves and God created by human sinfulness.

Baal: In Canaanite mythology, the god of fertility, worshiped as the one who controls the rains. Baal was one of the gods considered to be a principal enemy of God in the history of Israel and Judah.

blessing: A prayer of praise and adoration to God; also an act or a word bestowed by God.

Canaan: The land, located between Syria and Egypt, where the Israelites settled.

covenant: The permanent commitment made by God, who shows his love and mercy by giving the commandments to the people, who are to worship God alone and be obedient and faithful.

covet: In the Ten Commandments, to not only desire something that does not belong to you but also work to wrongfully acquire it.

exile: Most often used in the Old Testament to describe the exile of Judah in Babylon in the period from 587 BC to 539 BC.

faith: The concrete sense of God's total commitment to the people and their absolute trust in him.

Feast of Booths (Feast of Tabernacles): The eight-day celebration of the harvest in which the people are required to live in booths to commemorate God's protection during the time in the wilderness.

Fertile Crescent: The arc of land beginning in the lower part of the Tigris-Euphrates River Valley and moving north and west to present-day Turkey and then down along the Palestinian coast to Egypt.

Holy of Holies: The innermost room of the temple, in which the Ark of the Covenant is located, representing God's presence and the secure covenantal relationship between God and the people.

hope: The concrete sense of being confident of God's willingness and ability to fulfill the terms of the covenant.

Hyksos: Asiatic tribes who conquered northern Egypt and ruled between 1667 BC and 1559 BC. It is thought that these rulers welcomed Joseph and the rest of Jacob's family to Egypt.

idolatry: The worship of an image or a statue instead of the true God.

jealous: When used of God, communicates the unique and total commitment that God has made to the people. In this sense, it has also been translated "impassioned." In terms of human relationships, it can mean a sinful state of envy.

judge: A man or a woman in the Old Testament who has authority and is able to mediate arguments and restore justice.

justice: In the Old Testament, the chief characteristic of God, who is the sure defender of the poor and the oppressed. God's justice is based on the promises he made in the covenant.

love: In reference to God in the Old Testament, a sign of God's continuing fidelity to the people, described as "steadfast love."

manna: The food provided by God when the people are in the wilderness.

mark on Cain: The mark of protection that God gives Cain in spite of his murder of Abel.

mercy: The loving-kindness, loyalty, and faithfulness that God shows to the people; also an instance of God being moved to compassion for the people.

messiah: A person who is anointed as God's representative in matters concerning the chosen people.

Nazirite: A man or a woman who lives in a consecrated state through the person's own or his or her parents' choice. A Nazirite is to abstain from drinking wine or other alcoholic drinks, avoid cutting his hair while following the vow, and avoid going near a dead body.

Passover: The most important celebration in the Old Testament and Judaism, commemorating the liberation of the people from slavery in Egypt through the action of God.

poor: Those who lack either material or spiritual goods, especially those who have lost what they have because of injustice or oppression.

postexilic: The period of Jewish history after the return to Canaan from Babylon.

preexilic: The period of the history of Judah and Israel before they were conquered by Assyria and Babylon.

prophet: A witness to God who is called to proclaim the word of God to the people concerning their sinful behavior and its consequences for them.

redemption: In the Old Testament, the reestablishment of God's relationship with the people after they disobey, rebel against, or are unfaithful to him.

repentance: In the Old Testament, turning back or going over your steps so that the right way can be found. For the prophets, this process involved an interior conversion, as evident in one who is just, kind, and humble.

righteousness: In the Old Testament, the action of God leading people into a correct relationship with him and with one another; God's continued commitment to keeping the covenant relationship with the people.

sacrifice: The offering of a clean animal or vegetable that is either completely or partially destroyed by fire on an altar as an act of adoration to God.

Septuagint: The Greek translation of the Hebrew Scriptures, made in Alexandria for the Greek-speaking Jews in the Greek world and later used by the early church.

Shema: The Jewish profession of faith, asserting that the Lord is their God, the Lord alone. By reciting the Shema, the believer forms his personal devotion to God and expresses his willingness to accept the ethical responsibility of practicing the Law.

tree of the knowledge of good and evil: Tree in paradise by which God tests the loyalty of Adam and Eve.

wrath of God: Can be understood as a symbol of the distance between God's love and human sinfulness. Images of the wrath of God are always correlated with images of God's mercy and kindness, as God is "slow to anger, and abounding in steadfast love and faithfulness" (Exodus 34:6).

Suggested Reading

These commentaries and introductions are excellent resources for further study.

The Bible Today magazine (Liturgical Press)

The Collegeville Bible Commentary: Old Testament series (Liturgical Press): Includes handy short commentaries on individual books of the Old Testament.

God's Library: A Catholic Introduction to the World's Greatest Book, Joe Paprocki (Loyola Press, 2005): Gives a basic understanding of the Bible and how it is interpreted by Catholics.

Invitation to the Old Testament: A Catholic Approach to the Hebrew Scriptures, Alice Camille (ACTA, 2004): Offers an accessible introduction to key themes and passages of the Old Testament.

New Light from Old Stories: The Hebrew Scriptures for Today's World, Leslie J. Hoppe (Paulist, 2005): Shows how the biblical writers articulated their religious beliefs through the medium of story.

The New Jerome Biblical Commentary, edited by Raymond E. Brown, Joseph A. Fitzmyer, and Roland E. Murphy (Prentice Hall, 1989): Provides the general reader with biblical commentary in one volume.

Priests, Prophets, and Sages: Catholic Perspectives on the Old Testament, Leslie J. Hoppe (St. Anthony Messenger, 1984): Shows the value of the Old Testament in relationship to Jesus' proclamation of the Good News.

Reading the Old Testament: An Introduction, Lawrence Boadt (Paulist, 1984): Offers an excellent introduction to the Old Testament.

Six Weeks with the Bible books on the Old Testament (Loyola Press):

- *Amos, Hosea, Micah: A Call to Justice*, Joe Paprocki (2006).

- *Exodus: God to the Rescue*, Jeanne Kun (2002).

- *Genesis 1–11: God Makes a Start*, Kevin Perrotta (2001).

- *Genesis 12–23: Abraham and Sarah's Journey*, Kevin and Louise Perrotta (2002).

- *Genesis 25–33: Jacob's Blessing*, Kevin and Louise Perrotta (2003).

- *Genesis 37–50: Joseph the Dreamer*, Kevin and Louise Perrotta (2004).

- *Isaiah 40–55: Build a Highway for God*, Kevin Perrotta (2003).

- *Job: A Good Man Asks Why*, Kevin Perrotta (2001).

- *Jonah/Ruth: Love Crosses Boundaries*, Kevin Perrotta (2000).

- *On the Way to the Promised Land*, Kevin Perrotta (2006).

- *Psalms: An Invitation to Prayer*, Kevin Perrotta (2000).

- *Psalms II: Praying with Jesus*, Kevin Perrotta (2003).

- *Proverbs: Wisdom for Living*, Kevin Perrotta (2003).

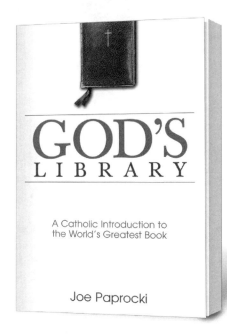

A Special Invitation

Loyola Press invites you to become one of our Loyola Press Advisors! Join our unique online community of people willing to share with us their thoughts and ideas about Catholic life and faith. By sharing your perspective, you will help us improve our books and serve the greater Catholic community.

From time to time, registered advisors are invited to participate in online surveys and discussion groups. Most surveys will take less than ten minutes to complete. Loyola Press will recognize your time and efforts with gift certificates and prizes. Your personal information will be held in strict confidence. Your participation will be for research purposes only, and at no time will we try to sell you anything.

Please consider this opportunity to help Loyola Press improve our products and better serve you and the Catholic community. To learn more or to join, visit **www.SpiritedTalk.org** and register today.

—THE LOYOLA PRESS ADVISORY TEAM